D0197867

MUCH
PRAYER
MUCH
POWER

PETER DEYNEKA

MUCH
PRAYER
MUCH
POWER

**CHANGE YOUR WORLD
THROUGH THE
POWER OF PRAYER**

CONTENTS

FOREWORD

Peter Deyneka was one of the great prayer warriors of the 20th century. He was born in 1898 in a small Belarussian village near the Yaseldah River, in the province of Grodno. There were eight children in the Deyneka family, and he was next to the eldest. When young Peter was just 15 years of age, his mother and father decided to send him to the United States to seek employment so that he might send money back to his family to help them buy food. On March 3, 1914, young Peter bid his family farewell. His father took him 25 miles on a wagon to the closest train station. There, he boarded the first train he had ever seen and was soon sailing from Libau on the Russian ocean liner *S.S. Dvinsk* to New York, where he caught a train to Chicago and began his new life.

He joined his cousin, Walter Markawitz, at a boarding house and soon found work in a lumber yard. One Sunday morning he encountered Russians singing and preaching the Gospel on a street corner in Chicago. Before long, a curious young Peter went to hear Billy Sunday preach, not knowing it would be a religious service. He heard about Christ, but did not understand. Then the Lord provided a room in a Russian Christian home where — to his great dismay — believers would come and pray for him. He fled to an American home, but the prayers of the Russian Christians followed him.

Peter heard about Moody Church and began to attend just so he could listen to and learn the English language without charge. On Sunday evening, January 18, 1920, Pastor Paul Rader preached a penetrating evangelistic message and gave an invitation for salvation. Peter answered the call and accepted the Lord Jesus Christ as his Savior. The next morning, he awakened a new creature in Christ and became a soul winner for the rest of his life. He joined the Ushers' Prayer Band at Moody Church. He could hardly wait until the next Sunday so that he could spend an hour with the brothers praying for souls to be saved.

He studied at Moody Bible Institute and went on to graduate from St. Paul Bible Institute in St. Paul, Minnesota. Following graduation, he was called to pastor in Clear Lake, Iowa. World War I had driven his family to central Russia and all contact had been lost. Finally, after long years of being separated, he heard from his mother who informed him that his family was dying of starvation. The famine had already taken the lives of three brothers and two sisters, and one brother had died before the war. The news devastated Peter, and he spent all night and the next day in prayer for his father, mother and surviving brother. Two days later, a Christian friend became burdened to give him money which he cabled directly to his family in Russia. As soon as possible, he returned to Russia only to learn that his father, who had wanted to hear about Christ, had passed away a few weeks earlier.

Peter began to travel and preach throughout Europe. He developed a tremendous burden for the souls of Russians and other Slavic-speaking peoples. After much prayer and waiting upon the Lord, God gave clear leading for him to launch out by faith and form a Gospel association to carry on a work among the Slavic peoples. Through prayer, the Russian Gospel Association, later renamed Slavic Gospel Association, was born in January 1934.

Over the years to follow, "Peter Dynamite," as he was affectionately called, became known throughout the world as a powerful evangelist and a great man of prayer. He would frequently be called upon to travel to the far corners of the globe to lead all-night prayer meetings in support of major evangelistic campaigns. Under his visionary leadership, SGA ministries were established in Canada, South America, Europe, Australia and New Zealand. Thousands of radio programs were broadcast *over* the Iron Curtain and millions of Bibles were discreetly delivered *under* the Iron Curtain, to encourage persecuted Christians and to bring the message of hope to countless lost souls. All of this was made possible by God's supply in answer to the faithful prayers of Peter Deyneka and his partners in the Gospel.

Jeremiah 33:3 says, "Call to Me, and I will answer you, and show you great and mighty things, which you do not know." This book tells how throughout Peter Deyneka Sr.'s life and ministry, much prayer resulted in much power! It is sure to strengthen the prayer life of every reader. May God richly bless you as you read it.

DR. ROBERT W. PROVOST
President of Slavic Gospel Association

PREFACE

This book was written after much prayer, because the Lord laid a heavy burden on my heart to prepare it. I was also asked by many friends throughout my travels to write a book about my experiences in how God answers prayer, how to start and conduct prayer meetings, and how to get others to pray.

My prayer is that God will use this book mightily for His glory, to encourage young people and others to pray, and to call many to become real prayer warriors — to pray much and receive great power and victory in their lives.

REV. PETER DEYNEKA
1898 – 1987
founder of Slavic Gospel Association

1

WHY PRAY?

The Bible, the holy Word of God, gives many reasons why we should pray. Yet many people do not think it is important or necessary to emphasize prayer. There are Christians who depend much on experience, education, works, effort, action and programs, yet leave out the most important thing in the Christian life — prayer. Some seldom pray. Others pray only when they feel like it. We are not to pray only when we feel like praying. According to the Word of God, prayer must be a regular, common practice in our lives. It is our spiritual breath and life. We cannot live spiritually without it.

CHRIST NEEDED TO PRAY — WE MUST PRAY

In Matthew 14:23 we read, "And when He had sent the multitudes away, He went up on the mountain by Himself to pray. Now when evening came, He was alone there." Just think, Jesus Christ, the Son of God, prayed and talked much, in private, to His Heavenly Father. If the Son of God prayed, how much more do we need to pray to our Heavenly Father! Jesus went alone to a mountain to pray. Any one of us can get alone to pray. It is important for each Christian to go some place where no one can disturb him and pour out his heart to God.

In Luke 5:16 we read, "So He Himself often withdrew into the wilderness and prayed." Jesus tried to separate Himself from all else to be alone in undisturbed prayer. If Jesus practiced this important type of prayer, we too should find a quiet place where we can really spend time in prayer.

Why pray? Because we cannot get along without prayer and maintain a healthy spiritual life, just as we cannot get along without food to keep our physical bodies going. In the same way, many Christians today are weak because of lack of prayer. They have no joy, no blessing, no power, no victory, and no desire to serve the Lord. If you do not make prayer a constant practice in your life, you will have no power in your life. If you do not have fellowship with God through prayer, you will find it hard to go through the physical and spiritual tests and trials of life. Christ is our example in this respect. He took much time to pray — we also must pray.

Christ expects all of us to be praying children. Prayer is a definite necessity.

CHRIST COMMANDED US TO PRAY

When Jesus had the great burden of His last days on earth on His heart, He took three of His disciples with Him to pray. He left them while He went farther into the garden to pray. It was a great disappointment to Jesus to find His followers asleep when He returned, instead of bearing His burden with Him. As He turned to go back into the garden to pray, He challenged them again to "watch and pray." But when He returned again, He found them asleep *again* . . .

> Then Jesus came with them to a place called Gethsemane, and said to the disciples, "Sit here while I go and pray over there." And He took with Him Peter and the two sons of Zebedee, and He began to be sorrowful and deeply distressed. Then He said to them, "My soul is exceedingly sorrowful, even to death. Stay here and watch with Me." He went a little farther and fell on His face, and prayed, saying, "O

> My Father, if it is possible, let this cup pass from Me;
> nevertheless, not as I will, but as You will." Then He
> came to the disciples and found them asleep, and
> said to Peter, "What? Could you not watch with Me
> one hour? Watch and pray, lest you enter into temp-
> tation. The spirit indeed is willing, but the flesh is
> weak" (Matthew 26:36-41).

Many believers today are sleeping spiritually, having no burden upon their hearts. This is why we have so little revival, joy, blessing and missionary vision. Many today actually do not want to be spiritually awakened or stirred to do something for God. The Bible says that where there is no vision, the people perish. If we continue to live lives of little prayer, our vision will remain small and we will not accomplish much for God. We must take time to pray and become burdened for God's work so He can use us in a new way and so we can see great things done for Him.

Why pray? "Lest you enter into temptation." Many today cannot resist temptation because they are not watching and praying. God is able to deliver anyone from temptation if he will only walk in prayer, in constant submission to God and His will. However, it seems to be a most difficult thing for people to see their need of constant prayer. The Bible says, "Therefore submit to God. Resist the devil and he will flee from you" (James 4:7). As our lives are constantly yielded to God in prayer, He has promised to give us the strength to resist the devil so that he will flee from us.

Before He left for heaven, Jesus gave what I believe to be one of His greatest commands: "Therefore pray the Lord of the harvest to send out laborers into His harvest" (Matthew 9:38). Christ commanded His disciples to pray. Thus, Christ also commands us to pray. Not all Christians can go to the mission field, preach, play an instrument, sing, or give large sums of money. But we can *all* pray! We must obey His command.

Have you prayed today for lost souls, for those who are in need, and for those who are ministering the Word of God? Few people these days are praying for the mission fields of the world. Not only did Christ tell us to pray, but He told us to pray that laborers would be sent into His harvest fields. This is a part all of us can have in missionary work. We can pray out more missionaries from our families and our churches. A missionary church is a praying church, and if it is a praying church, we find that it is also a giving church. One duty in which every Christian can and must have a part, without excuse, is prayer. Christ expects you and me to pray.

Not just those who preach the Gospel will receive rewards in heaven. Everyone who prays for pastors, missionaries, evangelists, Bible teachers, personal workers, Sunday school teachers, Gospel musicians and others will share in the rewards. May the command of the Lord challenge you to pray more than you ever have. Expect great things from God and undertake great things for Him. Be faithful in prayer.

When the late Paul Rader, well-known pastor and evangelist, was conducting Bible conferences at Lake Harbor, Michigan (Maranatha Bible Conference), he asked me to come there for two summers in 1930 and '31, to pray and get others to pray in the prayer tower which overlooks the Bible conference grounds on Lake Michigan. The tower was busy with the many people who came out to those prayer meetings which we had every morning and many evenings. Since there were so many people attending the Bible conference and so many needs to be met — hundreds of young people attending whose lives were needed for the Lord's work in different parts of the world, many thousands of dollars needed to send them out, many preachers whose messages were needed to challenge the people — Mr. Rader felt much prayer was necessary. The lives of many of those people who came to that prayer tower were spiritually changed as they saw a great new need for prayer in their own personal lives.

In 1920, when Paul Rader was conducting the Bible conference at Cedar Lake, Indiana, he would often announce a special men's prayer meeting in the woods. What glorious times of prayer and challenge we had as we met God among those trees. Mr. Rader was a great man of prayer. He knew that prayer was necessary if the meetings were going to accomplish what they should and if lives were going to be challenged.

BY PRAYER WE TALK TO GOD

Praying is simply talking to God from your heart, directing your thoughts and words to Him. God talks to us as we read the Bible. We talk to Him as we pray. *Both* are very important.

Prayer is just like talking to a friend. It is not necessary to prepare a great speech. God understands us in our simplicity and desires to hear from all of His children. It pleases the Father when we talk to Him. Just like a father and mother are pleased when their children come to them, telling of their love and needs, so our Heavenly Father is also pleased when we come to Him with our joys, burdens, cares and whatever may be upon our hearts.

God gave us a wonderful promise in Jeremiah 33:3 when He said: "Call to Me, and I will answer you, and show you great and mighty things, which you do not know." Just think . . . God tells us to call upon Him, just like a good friend would ask you to call him when you are in need. Isn't that wonderful? God said He would not only answer us, but show us mighty things about which we know nothing. God has many blessings and victories in store for those who will take time to talk to Him.

It is no problem to talk to someone whom you love dearly. No one has to force you to do this; you do it willingly and gladly. We should come to God with even greater joy for the wonderful privilege of talking to Him. He is our best friend. He understands every single thing about us. He knows every problem we have. And He promised in His Word: "I will never leave you, nor forsake you."

GOD IS WORTHY OF OUR PRAISE

Since God has created this great universe and all of the people in it, and since He has control of the affairs of all nations and people, He wants to hear praise and thanks from His children as they realize His love toward them in creating them, saving them, and directing their lives by the wisdom of His will. God wants to hear our love, adoration and worship of Him as we come to Him with prayers of deep, grateful appreciation for all that He is and has done for us.

Anna served God night and day, worshiping Him by means of her prayers. "And this woman was a widow of about 84 years, who did not depart from the temple, but served God with fastings and prayers night and day" (Luke 2:37). She pleased God for many years by taking time to worship, adore and thank Him through her prayers. David also often worshiped God in prayer, as we see recorded in his psalms.

God can use anyone through prayer. I believe that God is not only still looking for men and women through whom He can work in a more active service among people, but also for those who will take time to get alone and serve Him by means of their thanksgiving and adoration. It is a wonderful thing to tell the Lord that we love Him and thank Him for saving our souls, for blessing us, for helping us, for supplying our every need, and for all of His mercies and goodness which are showered upon His people. This pleases Him because it shows that we love Him. We must continually thank God for all of His kindness and care for all of His children.

WE MUST INTERCEDE FOR OTHERS THROUGH PRAYER

The Word of God commands us to pray for one another. James 5:16 says, "Confess your trespasses to one another, and pray for one another, that you may be healed. The effective, fervent prayer of a righteous man avails much." It is the righteous man, the spiritual man, the man who walks with God and has communion and fellowship with our Lord Jesus Christ,

18

whose prayer avails much. This verse tells us that we should pray for one another concerning our physical needs. The Lord is able to heal the body, as we pray for His will to be done.

In 1 Samuel 7, Samuel told Israel to gather together and he would pray to God for the people. Samuel was concerned for his brethren and very willing to pray for them that God's will would be accomplished. Paul says in Galatians 6:2, "Bear one another's burdens, and so fulfill the law of Christ." The Lord expects that we should pray and be concerned for one another. Whenever we pray for others, the Lord blesses us. Some people have the habit of praying only for themselves.

I once heard a man give a brokenhearted testimony. Although he had a little five-year-old girl named Mary, whenever this man prayed he only remembered his wife and himself. One morning after praying for his wife and himself during their devotional time, Mary came up to him and put her little arms around him and said, "Daddy, ask the Lord to bless me too." He broke down and wept, asking God to forgive him.

It is important to pray for our children. There are many children who are unsaved today because parents have failed to pray for them and with them. Often only after these children grow up, leave home, and begin to live their own lives apart from God do the parents begin to cry with broken hearts of concern because their children are unsaved and out in the world. It is so important to have a family altar where you pray together with your children and for them — *before* the children grow up and leave home!

How my wife and I thank God that we had the privilege and joy of having a family prayer time from the beginning of our life together. God heard our prayers regarding our children. We had the joy of leading all three of them to our Lord and Savior, Jesus Christ. I also had the joy of baptizing them. All three dedicated their lives for the Lord's service, received training in Christian colleges, and went on to serve Him in their respective fields. We urge all parents to pray for their children.

Husbands and wives should begin praying together at the start of their marriage so that God will guide and bless their new life, in every phase, from the very beginning. God should have first place in the life of every Christian couple. Jesus says in Matthew 6:33, "But seek first the kingdom of God and His righteousness, and all these things shall be added to you."

It pleases God that we not only pray for one another, but also for leaders and all who are in authority in the government of our land. 1 Timothy 2:1-3 says, "Therefore I exhort first of all that supplications, prayers, intercessions, and giving of thanks be made for all men, for kings and all who are in authority, that we may lead a quiet and peaceable life in all godliness and reverence. For this is good and acceptable in the sight of God our Savior." I fear that sometimes we do not pray enough for the heads of our government. I was greatly impressed, while attending the President's Prayer Breakfast in Washington, D.C., when I heard some of our great leaders praying and seeking God's will and help in the guidance of our country. I believe that God blesses America because of this, and we ought to pray all the more for our leaders, that they might do the will of God in dealing with national and international affairs.

OUR NEEDS ARE SUPPLIED THROUGH PRAYER

Hebrews 4:16 tells us, "Let us therefore come boldly to the throne of grace, that we may obtain mercy and find grace to help in time of need." The Lord tells us to come boldly to Him — without fear, without doubt, without hesitation — in order that He might help us in our time of need. This invitation is open to every Christian in any place at any time. In this New Testament age, we have a new and living way of entrance to God. There are no more sacrifices or rituals necessary to be performed for our worship. We are now priests of God because of what Christ has done. As His priests and children, we can come to Him any time we have a need. That is God's desire. It is our privilege and opportunity to take advantage of this.

In this same respect, Jesus said, "Ask, and it will be given to you; seek, and you will find; knock, and it will be opened to you. For everyone who asks receives, and he who seeks finds, and to him who knocks it will be opened" (Matthew 7:7-8). The Lord has told us to ask, seek and knock through prayer. When we lose something, we are determined to look until we find it. Likewise, we should be determined in our praying to continue asking and knocking until our needs are supplied.

When I was saved in 1920 at Moody Church in Chicago, I asked God to make me a prayer warrior. I didn't know much about praying, but I began to pray anyway. I thank God that throughout all of these years He has given me a burden of prayer through which I have found great comfort and the supply of all my needs. Before Slavic Gospel Association was established in 1934, we spent much time in prayer and fasting, wondering how God would lead and supply all the needs for such a great work. The Lord heard our prayers, directed my life, began that missionary organization, and has performed great miracles. Prayer is real.

In Luke 6:12, we see that Jesus went to a mountain and continued in prayer all night to God. Early the next morning, after much prayer, He called His followers to Him and from that group chose 12 apostles whom He would teach and send out to preach. So often we choose first, then pray. It is much better to pray first, that God would definitely lead before we act or make any decisions. We must not pray that God will supply our wants, but that He will supply our needs. God does not always give us what we would like to have, but God does supply all of our needs in answer to our cries.

We have no strength in ourselves. We cannot be spiritual by depending merely on education, experience, personality or past works. We must depend entirely on the Holy Spirit in order to be men and women of God. May the Lord help us to pray earnestly, as Christ did, so that we may be kept spiritual, powerful and growing in the grace of our Lord Jesus Christ.

2

MUCH PRAYER

Jesus prayed much. We read in Mark 6:46-47, "And when He had sent them away, He departed to the mountain to pray. Now when evening came, the boat was in the middle of the sea; and He was alone on the land." Jesus separated Himself from the crowds to get alone. He prayed even into the late hours. Christ prayed much alone! There is a time to pray together with two or three, or in a church prayer meeting, but there are also many times when the Christian needs to get alone with God — not just to say a prayer, but to pray much.

Before His betrayal, Jesus had a heavy heart. He took much time for prayer in the garden of Gethsemane (Luke 22:39-44). How much time do you spend alone in prayer with God? Are you giving some of your time to God daily, so that He might have an opportunity to speak to you through His Word as you read the Bible and pray? Whenever we spend time in prayer, it is an opportunity for God to show us more of His will for our lives. If you want to have much power, blessing and victory, you must spend much time in prayer.

PRAY WITHOUT CEASING

We are told in 1 Thessalonians 5:17 to "pray without ceasing." This does not mean that we must be on our knees all of the time, but it does mean that we should be in the spirit of prayer no matter where we are or what we are doing. When our minds are occupied with prayer, we have constant close fellowship with God so that we might know the mind of Christ and learn His will for every situation.

In Luke 18:1, Jesus explained that "men always ought to pray and not lose heart." Not only are we to take time from a busy day to pray, but we are to be praying in spirit all day long. When we have this constant fellowship with God in prayer, we are stronger spiritually. This is not only a command or responsibility which we have from Christ, but it is a privilege, joy and blessing to be able to pray.

In 1 Samuel 12:23 we read, "Far be it from me that I should sin against the Lord in ceasing to pray for you." We learn from God's Word that *not* praying is sin. In the Russian-language Bible this verse is translated, "I will not permit myself to sin before God by ceasing to pray for you." A person who does not pray is sinning, yet how many professing Christians today do not see the necessity and importance of prayer!

Jesus gave us two more stories which show the importance of continued prayer. The first is found in Luke 11:5-10. A man went to his friend at midnight and asked him for three loaves of bread. The friend told him not to bother him because he and his family had gone to bed for the night. But the man kept asking for the loaves until he got them from his friend. Because of the man's persistence, his friend gave him the bread. Jesus is teaching us here that we should have this same attitude and spirit of urgency in our praying.

In the second story, which is given in Luke 18:1-8, Jesus tells of a judge in a certain city, who feared neither man nor God. A woman kept coming to him, asking for help. He did not want to respond, but because she persisted he decided to help her. He said, "Because this widow troubles me I will avenge her, lest by her continual coming she weary me."

Jesus said that God would also hear those who keep coming to Him with a particular request: "And shall God not avenge

His own elect who cry out day and night to Him, though He bears long with them?" This is our example for prayer. We should not stop praying for our problems and needs.

Many people like to talk about the great prayer meetings they used to have or about the powerful periods of time they used to spend with God. But today they are too busy to take time to experience these things. We do not depend on the good meals we had years ago for our physical strength today. We must take time to eat every day to maintain our physical strength. Likewise, God wants us to take time to talk to Him every day. Great men of God whom we have known, who have been used by Him, have been great men of prayer. You too can know God and be used by Him as you never have before. Begin to take more time to talk to Him. Any time of the day or night, you can be in a spirit of prayer quietly before God.

In my travels around the world, I have seen and learned that there are many gods made by hands. These gods are the objects of worship and prayer for many millions of people. These people are worshiping idols and praying to dead gods, yet many of them are faithful in their prayers. Although they are living in darkness and sin, spiritually lost and blinded, they put many Christians to shame by their devotion and consecration. We believe in sending out missionaries to tell these people of the good news of the living Christ who hears and answers prayer, but while we are doing this we should check our own lives to see how much devotion, faith and trust we have in the living God.

In John 15:5 Jesus said, ". . . for without Me you can do nothing." It is very plain that without God's help we will be unable to accomplish anything for Him. As we realize this, we are compelled to depend more and more upon God's answers to our prayers for the needs and problems that we face and for help to solve them. We know that only the living, true God answers prayer. He is the only One who can help. And because we believe He answers prayer, we come to Him in faith.

Are we as Christians trusting in the true God, taking time to talk to our God in prayer? Do we love Him enough to desire to be with Him in constant fellowship throughout our prayers? As we come to Him, He not only wants to hear about our needs, problems and requests, but He also deserves our worship and adoration. He wants to receive that from us by means of our praise and thanksgiving directed to Him.

NECESSITY AND RESPONSIBILITY OF CHRISTIANS TO PRAY

The disciples in the early church realized the necessity of much prayer. They appointed men to look after the needs of the people so they could give themselves to prayer. We read in Acts 6:4, "But we will give ourselves continually to prayer and to the ministry of the Word." Every Christian worker must spend time in prayer. Everyone who has been used mightily of God has been a person of prayer. They spent many hours in prayer. Some, such as D. L. Moody, C. T. Studd, Hudson Taylor, George Mueller and many others, rose early in the morning to meet God in prayer. Because they prayed much, God gave them much power, wisdom and victory. God is using men who are on their faces before Him. When there is much prayer, there is much victory and much success in Christian work. If Christian workers do not take time to pray, they will lack the power of God no matter how talented or gifted they might be. We must be praying men and women.

We know there are many Christian workers in Russia today who prayed much in the past during times of great difficulty and who continue to pray now. That is why Christianity is spreading and why there are revivals in various places in Russia. God is honoring their prayers and witness for Him.

The Lord laid the burden of the importance of prayer on my heart right after my conversion. The first time I prayed publicly was at Moody Church in Chicago, at the ushers' prayer meeting held each Sunday morning before Sunday school. We prayed for God's blessing on the Sunday school teachers and the pastor. It was there I saw that the secret of power in a Christian's life was through much sincere prayer. I asked God to make me a real prayer warrior. My greatest desire became to wait on the Lord no matter where I am — at home, traveling by plane, train, bus, car, or walking. I want to be praying constantly for God's guidance and to be used for His glory.

PRAY MUCH DURING PERSECUTION AND PROBLEMS

Many Christians today feel they are in God's will and praise the Lord only when things run smoothly or come easily to them without any difficulty or opposition. God's Word tells us not only to rejoice when everything is well, but even during sorrow and tribulation. "But even if you should suffer for righteousness' sake, you are blessed. And do not be afraid of their threats, nor be troubled" (1 Peter 3:14). We should rejoice in *all* things. The Lord allows them to come into our lives for our good. During times of persecution and opposition we should pray much, asking the Lord for strength to be victorious. Many Christians have been drawn closer to the Lord during times of testing because they realized more than ever their need for total, constant dependence upon the Lord for help and strength.

Even though Daniel knew a decree had been signed that forbade praying to any god except the king of the land, he continued to fearlessly pray as much as he always had. "Now when Daniel knew that the writing was signed, he went home. And in his upper room, with his windows open toward Jerusalem, he knelt down on his knees three times that day, and prayed and gave thanks before his God, as was his custom since early days" (Daniel 6:10). Daniel was not ashamed or afraid to pray even though he knew it would bring about difficulties for him. Prayer was as necessary to him as eating or sleeping.

Have you ever been ashamed to pray because you felt it might embarrass you or cause people to talk about you? We do not need to fear man or be ashamed to pray when others might hear us. God honors those who are not ashamed of Him and those who are depending entirely upon Him through prayer. How wonderful it is to have an opportunity to pour out our hearts to God in prayer like Daniel did.

In Daniel 3, three Hebrew children were thrown into a fiery furnace. They were not burned because the Lord was with them. God can protect men and women in spite of their suffering and persecution. When it seems that everyone is turning against us, Romans 8:31 gives us the promise: "If God is for us, who can be against us?"

Prayer was one of the most important things in Daniel's life. He did not stop praying because of opposition. In times like those we should seek the Lord for encouragement. Any man or woman who is being used of God will be criticized and opposed. Someone will always find fault. Jealousy and criticism creep into one's life so easily, especially toward those whom God is mightily using. These are terrible sins that come into the lives of some Christians. Christ never did harm to anyone, yet He was persecuted by those who despised Him. "He was oppressed and He was afflicted, yet He opened not His mouth; He was led as a lamb to the slaughter, and as a sheep before its shearers is silent, so He opened not His mouth" (Isaiah 53:7).

I shall never forget some experiences I had in Belarus when I visited my home and family for the first time after I had been saved. My mother professed to have religion, but did not know Christ as her personal Savior. Because of this, I met great opposition and persecution right in my own home. My mother was convinced that in two weeks I would stop preaching the Gospel and cease following the Lord. She wanted me to go back into the type of life I formerly lived. I told her that since Christ had saved me, I belonged to Him and no one could ever make me turn back to the sinful life I had lived. I was a new creature in Christ and had passed from death unto life — a new life in Him. "Therefore, if anyone is in Christ, he is a new creation;

old things have passed away; behold, all things have become new" (2 Corinthians 5:17).

For nearly a year, I had to endure suffering for the Gospel's sake in my home. The more I prayed for my mother, the more disturbed she became. This showed me that the Holy Spirit was working in her heart. So I kept on praying. When I returned to the United States, my mother was still unsaved. But I continued praying for her salvation. Humanly speaking, it looked as if she would never turn to Christ. It seemed impossible, but my hope was in Christ.

When I returned home again, after many years of much prayer, my mother met me with open arms. Even before I got to the house she cried out, "Peter, I've given my heart to Christ." There, while we were greeting one another, she broke down and wept for joy because she had now accepted Christ as her Savior. Thank God, my mother was saved! If you have an unsaved father, mother, children, relatives or friends whom you want to see come to Christ, keep on praying in spite of any suffering or persecution. Be faithful in prayer.

Once during my travels in Europe, a lady came to me crying and said she had been saved for many years but was enduring great persecution from her husband. As a result, she had no patience with him and did not feel like praying for him because he was an atheist. I told her that she should stop preaching to him and start praying — God would change her and save her husband. She did, and in three months God answered her prayer, revived her heart, and saved her husband.

There are thousands of families where some members are Christians and others are not. In these cases, many have been persecuted because they try to witness for the Lord. The most important thing is to live an exemplary life and pray for your loved ones. You must have patience, not saying anything that would grieve the Lord or be a stumbling block to the unsaved. "Let your light so shine before men, that they may see your good works and glorify your Father in heaven" (Matthew 5:16).

Many make the mistake of thinking that by debating or arguing they can bring another person to Christ. We cannot lead a person to Christ in this way. Only the Holy Spirit can convict a person of sin and bring him to accept Christ.

When my wife accepted the Lord as her personal Savior, before we were married, she was greatly opposed by her parents because she decided to follow the living Christ. Her parents professed to be religious but did not know Christ as their Savior. They often tried to keep her from attending church services. She went through much persecution, opposition and trials. The only thing she could do for her parents was to pray for them. God heard her prayers. After several years of prayer, patience and love, her father and mother accepted Christ as their Savior and both were baptized. We cannot live by feelings — we must walk by faith, trusting Him for the victory. "Faith is the victory that overcomes the world."

Another time when I was traveling in Eastern Europe, one of our Russian preachers who had been imprisoned for the Gospel's sake told me, "Brother Deyneka, although it does not feel so good when we are going through persecution and suffering, we know it is good for us." I have known many others who have suffered greatly. One of the many refugees I've met told me that he was in Siberia for the Gospel's sake and there suffered great persecution in the labor camps. He said he never asked the Lord why He allowed this to happen to him, but always praised God and had victory in his heart because he knew he was going through trials for the Lord. He prayed that the Lord would give him strength to endure it all as a testimony for God. During this time of persecution, Christ became more real than ever before in his life.

After I was saved and went back to my home in Russia, I not only had much opposition from my mother but also from my only brother. He was ashamed to walk through the village with me because I believed in God. He was an atheist and very ungodly, but I prayed for him for many years. On my last journey from my parents' home to the States, he was walking with me to see me off. Before saying goodbye to him, I said, "Andrew, what shall I say to my friends in the United States? That you have remained an atheist, or that you have accepted Christ as your Savior?" Tears filled his eyes, and after a little while he told me that the more I prayed for him, the worse he felt and the more he suffered, even physically. Through prayer, God broke his stubborn heart and changed his life.

A NIGHT OF PRAYER

We find in God's Word that He gives mighty victory to those who pray earnestly. Many have experienced great victories because of nights of prayer. Jesus prayed all night. If He saw the necessity for this, how much more do we need to pray! By setting yourself apart from the world and its cares and praying during the quiet hours of the night, you can get alone with God and give the Holy Spirit an opportunity to work in and through you. When Peter was thrown into jail for preaching the Gospel, the Christians prayed into the night for his release. "Peter was therefore kept in prison, but constant prayer was offered to God for him by the church" (Acts 12:5). God heard their prayer. When the answer came, they could hardly believe that Peter had already been released.

Even though Paul and Silas were persecuted, beaten and suffered much for the Gospel's sake, we read in Acts 16:25-26 that they prayed and sang praises unto God while they were bound in prison. God heard their prayer and immediately sent an earthquake which shook the foundation of the prison and they were set free. When Paul prayed, he believed God and saw things happen. If we believe Him when we pray and praise Him by faith because He hears our prayers, we will have real liberty, joy, blessing and victory in our hearts. Even though outward circumstances may be difficult, the Lord will give us the strength to endure them and be victorious.

Nehemiah 1:6 says, "Let Your ear be attentive and Your

eyes open, that You may hear the prayer of Your servant which I pray before You now, day and night, for the children of Israel Your servants, and confess the sins of the children of Israel which we have sinned against You. Both my father's house and I have sinned." What a confession Nehemiah made! God honors anyone who humbles himself and confesses his need. Nehemiah said he was praying day and night for the children of Israel. A deep burden for others always results in much prayer. We should pray day and night for our friends and relatives, that they too might be saved. We should pray for revival in our churches and mission fields. I believe that one of the greatest sins in a Christian's life is prayerlessness, not taking time to pray or read the Word of God. Saying a prayer just to quiet our conscience is not enough. We must take time to wait upon the Lord and renew our strength.

Genesis 32:24-26 tells us that Jacob was alone, wrestling all night with a man from God. Jacob would not let go until God blessed him. Sometimes the Lord answers our prayers immediately, and sometimes He puts us through a test of our faith. Some prayers take time to be answered, but we should never give up. If it is according to His will, we will receive that for which we ask. He knows what is best for us. The Lord sometimes sends tests and trials our way so we might realize we have to wrestle and really wait on God in prayer day and night. I believe that these times of waiting on Him were one of the greatest things in my life in the beginning of my Christian work for the Lord.

Over the years I have led many all-night prayer meetings in many parts of the world, including the Youth for Christ conventions in Europe, South America and North America. I have seen God's power manifested in such a way that many yielded their lives to Him. Many ministers of the Gospel and other Christians have been changed because of the long hours of prayer through the night. At evangelistic and missionary conventions, Bible conferences and youth rallies, we have had all-night prayer meetings. Many, for whom this was their first experience, said they would never forget it. Because of these all-night prayer meetings, God gave them a burden for souls and a deeper desire to serve Him.

PERSEVERING PRAYER

In 1922, I received the first letter in five years from my parents, who were in central Russia at the time. My mother and father wrote that the family was dying from starvation. Three of my brothers and two sisters had already died as a result of famine, leaving one brother, my father and mother. My heart was greatly moved because they had died without hearing much about the love of Christ.

I spent a day and night in prayer for my parents, desiring to help them in their great need. My appetite was gone, sleep was gone, but I had a hungry heart to talk to the Lord. Like Jacob, I did not give up until the Lord blessed me and I believed that God was going to do something. The next morning, a Christian friend came to see me and said that because of a great burden she had for me she could not sleep during the past night. She thought I had some need, so she came over to give me some money that perhaps could be sent to someone in Russia to help buy food. I asked her how she knew I had this great need, and she said, "The Lord laid it on my heart and I felt there must be a need." Praise the Lord. He heard my cry and money was given me to immediately send to my parents in Russia so they could buy food.

Before my first missionary trip in 1925, soon after I graduated from Bible school, I started to pray and seek God's will as to when I should go to Eastern Europe with the Gospel and visit my parents on the borders of Russia. After spending some time waiting on the Lord in prayer, He wonderfully answered and provided enough money for my trip and support for almost the whole year that I would be in Belarus. Not only that, the Lord also sent enough extra funds so that I could help the poor and needy with clothing and food, and also build a chapel in which the Gospel was preached for many years.

Slavic Gospel Association was born through prayer and fasting in 1934, and we have continued through the years in much prayer to God for His continued guidance and blessing. From time to time, we spend a day in prayer at the SGA offices, in addition to our regular daily time of prayer. We experience great blessings and great results from these meetings. After prayer, we always notice how God blesses — souls are saved, workers are encouraged, and funds for the work are supplied.

Are you seeking God's will for your life? If you ask God in prayer to show you and are determined to put Him first in your life, He has promised that His Spirit of truth will lead you into truth. He will answer your prayers and guide you to the place where He wants you. As you continue to pray and look to Him in every phase of your life, He will supply every need along your pathway and give you the happiest life possible. I have found that to be very true in my own life. I am personally convinced that much prayer is a necessity for the Christian. You too can be a prayer warrior.

3

MUCH POWER

I have heard people jokingly say, "Why pray when you can worry." It is sad that this is so often the truth. If we would trust God instead of ourselves we would say, "Why worry when you can pray." You say that you do pray? Yes, you may have prayed, but have you prayed in faith, trusting God for His answer? If you have prayed in faith, trusting Him with real confidence, you do not have to worry. But if you pray with fear and doubt, then you worry and have not prayed in faith.

In Mark 11:22-24, Jesus said: "Have faith in God. For assuredly, I say to you, whoever says to this mountain, 'Be removed and be cast into the sea,' and does not doubt in his heart, but believes that those things he says will be done, he will have whatever he says. Therefore I say to you, whatever things you ask when you pray, believe that you receive them, and you will have them."

We can view all our trials, tribulations, problems, disappointments and discouragements as the high mountains which Jesus spoke about concerning prayer. When we pray, we should say to all of our problems, troubles and oppositions which come along, "Be removed and be cast into the sea." Yet some people have such terrific problems, sorrows and disappointments that they just refuse to pray, or say they cannot pray. They do not have strength or faith enough to pray. But notice that Jesus said we could say to the mountains, "Be removed." We must not doubt in our hearts when we ask something of God. If we are continually doubting and have no faith, our prayer is in vain.

Faith is important. We must have faith in God when we come to Him in prayer, because without faith we cannot please God. We read in Hebrews 11:6, "But without faith it is impossible to please Him, for he who comes to God must believe that He is, and that He is a rewarder of those who diligently seek Him." I believe the reason that many people pray and do not seem to get an answer is because they pray with fear, doubt and feelings — not in faith. A person can pray day and night, but if he does not believe that God is the One who answers prayer and can answer his particular prayer, that prayer does not get very far.

Jesus said to His disciples in Mark 11, "Have faith in God." Notice that Jesus tells us we must believe God. We must have confidence in God. As children come to their parents in simple faith and confidence, believing that their parents will help them and reply to whatever need they have, so we as children of God must come to Him in faith and expect that God will hear and answer us. However, just as parents do not always give their children whatever they ask for, because they know what is best for their children, I believe that God does the same because He knows what is best for you and me. He will not withhold any good thing from them that walk uprightly. He may not give us exactly that for which we ask because He knows it may not be best for us. Yet we know that God always answers prayer. He may answer yes, no, or wait — but He *does* answer our prayer according to His will.

Jesus went on to say, "Therefore I say to you, whatever things you ask when you pray, believe that you receive them, and you will have them." Isn't that a wonderful promise! If we really desire God's will when we pray, God clearly shows us in His Word that we can come to Him as His children in simple faith and believe Him for the answer. He wants us to know His will for every part of our life and His answer for every one of our problems. We receive these answers only when we have faith as we pray. It is necessary that we believe God can and will show us His solution to our requests as we come to Him in prayer. Faith in God and in His will while we are praying is absolutely necessary. Robert Hall once said, "The prayer of faith is the only power in the universe to which the great Jehovah yields. Prayer is the sovereign remedy."

I believe that Christ really commands us to believe as we pray. He says in Matthew 21:22, "And whatever things you ask in prayer, believing, you will receive." I am so glad that in prayer we can ask God concerning anything and everything. We must do it in real faith, believing Him, for only then do we receive the answer. The promise is that "ye will receive." Oh, may the Lord stir our hearts to believe Him, believe His Word, rest, have confidence in His promises, and thank Him for blessing and working in our lives through His answers to our prayers.

"If you can believe, all things are possible to him who believes" (Mark 9:23). Jesus told the man whose son needed help that the problem wasn't whether God could help his boy. There was no doubt that God could. The problem was whether or not the man *believed* that God could help the boy. Therefore Jesus told him that "all things are possible to him who believes." Can you believe today that God hears and answers prayer? Even your prayer? Jesus said that all things are possible to him who believes — not to him who merely hopes, or feels, or figures it out in his own mind as to how things may turn out, or whether it is possible, but to him who believes God.

I have had many experiences where I've asked a pastor if we could pray before the service and he has said, "No, it's not necessary. I'm preparing and thinking about the service." It is one thing to prepare and think, but it is also extremely important to pray that the Lord will anoint you for the service and that the Holy Spirit will work in the meeting. We should be much in prayer whenever we attempt to preach the Word of God. Unless we believe and trust God, we will not see much happening in our Christian lives or ministry.

There is a wonderful song written by Paul Rader entitled *Only Believe*. This song has been a blessing to many thousands of hearts and sung in many churches in many languages throughout the world . . .

> Fear not, little flock, whatever your lot,
> He enters all rooms, the doors being shut.
> He never forsakes, He never is gone,
> So count on His presence in darkness and dawn.
> Only believe, only believe;
> All things are possible, only believe.
> Only believe, only believe;
> All things are possible, only believe.

In the work of SGA, which is a worldwide missionary work among Russian-speaking people, much faith is exercised. There is no earthly guarantee for the financial support of the work, yet so many thousands of dollars are needed every month to send out to church workers located in many parts of the world. There are many who have no pledge for their support. Yet we trust God every day to send money in order to support them. There are many tests, and we often experience times when we are very low financially. During these times, we call for special prayer meetings aside from our regular daily time of prayer in the office. We take a few extra hours for prayer or have a whole day of prayer, trusting God, believing that He is going to hear our prayer and supply the need. God has performed miracles because we trust Him and ask in faith.

As we read the life stories of men who have been used by God, both in the past and in the present, we see that they were not only men of prayer, but men of faith.

MEN OF FAITH

We read in Daniel 3:28 that because the three young men trusted and had faith in God, they walked right in the midst of the fiery furnace yet were not harmed. Why? Because they trusted in the living God and God was with them. Their faith changed the king's mind toward them and won a victory for God. It does not matter how the enemy tries to make it hot and troublesome for you and me. When we trust God and have faith in Him, no harm shall be done unto us. No persecution or opposition shall separate us from God and His will for our lives. When we have fellowship with God and walk with Him, God the Holy Spirit walks with us no matter where we go.

Do you have any problems or trials? Then read Daniel 3 and see how God protected three men who trusted Him and saved them from all harm. Daniel prayed to God three times a day and was thrown into the lions' den because of it. What a wonderful testimony Daniel gave from the bottom of the lions' den as he looked up and spoke to the king saying, "My God sent His angel and shut the lions' mouths, so that they have not hurt me, because I was found innocent before Him; and also, O king, I have done no wrong before you" (Daniel 6:22). Surely the king was convinced that God protects His own. Just as Daniel was thrown among the lions and God shut the lions' mouths so they could not harm him, even today God can shut the mouths of our enemies in many ways so they cannot harm us. Often, the more we are persecuted by our enemies, the more we pray and the more God blesses us. Daniel was a man of faith and prayer, and God mightily led him because He believed God. Because Daniel continued to honor and trust God, he was delivered even from lions, as well as his enemies. God *can* help and deliver you from fiery trials and give you victory.

Hebrews 11:33-40 tells us that through a vital living faith, Enoch, Noah, Abraham, Joseph, Moses, David, Samuel and all the prophets won victories, brought about righteousness, obtained promises, stopped the mouths of lions, out of weakness were made strong, were persecuted for God, etc.-— but *never* gave up. Their faith, trust and strength was in God and not in themselves. Elijah prayed in faith when he prayed that it might not rain. Then again he prayed for rain, and it rained. He believed that God could do this and the Lord honored his faith and answered his prayer. He was a man like you and me, praying to the same God you and I know. The same almighty God can honor your faith today and give you joy, victory and strength such as you have never known before if you only put your whole trust in Him.

God said in Jeremiah 33:3, "Call to Me, and I will answer you, and show you great and mighty things, which you do not know." Notice this wonderful, powerful promise on prayer in the Bible. God said for us to call unto Him, pray unto Him, and He would answer us. This is a definite promise. It is a very plain promise from God that He will hear our cry. God says that if we do our part in praying, He will do His part in showing us great and mighty things. Even better than that, God promised that we would receive things we never even thought about or expected to have because we have called upon Him. In 2 Corinthians 5:7 we read, "For we walk by faith, not by sight." God reminds us that we must walk by faith, pray by faith, and expect answers by faith, to receive from Him great and mighty things.

James 5:17-18 says, "Elijah was a man with a nature like ours, and he prayed earnestly that it would not rain; and it did not rain on the land for three years and six months. And he prayed again, and the heaven gave rain, and the earth produced its fruit." We learn a few more details in 1 Kings 18:41-45. Elijah went to the top of Mount Carmel, cast himself down upon the earth, and hid his face between his knees as he prayed for rain. He sent his servant to see if there were any rain clouds. The servant returned and said there were none. Elijah told him seven times to go and look for clouds. Elijah continued to pray.

The seventh time the servant went to look, he saw a small cloud and in a short time it rained.

When Elijah prayed, he prayed earnestly and with a purpose. Elijah prayed specifically that God would stop the rain — and He did. Elijah earnestly prayed again that God would send rain — and He did. I believe that we should pray precisely and to the point. A person going to the store for groceries does not spend the day there asking for everything in the store. That person has a specific order for the things needed and the order is filled. When praying, ask for exactly those things which you need. Do not stop praying. Keep on asking and believing, and the Lord will supply your order according to His will.

Can we receive answers to our prayers today, even as the Old Testament prophets did? Yes, we can. The God of Elijah is the same One who hears and answers our prayers in this age.

After Prayer the Rain Stopped

Several years ago I was conducting evangelistic meetings in Argentina. The country's heavy rains made it difficult to get around when traveling in areas distant from the larger cities. It began raining on a Saturday morning near the conclusion of our special meetings. We had planned a united meeting in the central part of the province on Sunday morning, in the largest church in the district. Several hundred people were expected to attend and three choirs were to provide music.

It rained all day Saturday and people thought they would not be able to have a meeting the next day because of bad roads. That Saturday, we had a long service in the church. People did not want to go home. I cannot describe how wonderfully the Holy Spirit worked in our midst. As it continued to rain, the roads were becoming extremely muddy. I said to the people, "Before you go home, let us ask God — if it is His will — to stop the rain at least until noon tomorrow so we can have the united meeting." After our prayer, the rain stopped. On Sunday morning, the sun came out and the roads began to dry.

Two trucks provided transportation for the choir and the young people and we started on our way to the appointed place which was about 25 miles away. We had an inspiring meeting. Many became believers, and Christians were stirred and revived.

The weather was beautiful until about 1:00 p.m. After that, the rain came again. How it rained! The people began to say, "Brother Deyneka, you prayed that there would be no rain for half a day and that is exactly what happened! Why didn't you pray that there would be no rain for the entire day?" God answers prayer.

I will never forget another incident when the Lord stopped the rain in answer to prayer. Years ago, when Dr. Torrey M. Johnson was director of Chicagoland Youth for Christ, a special Youth for Christ rally was to be held at Chicago's huge Soldier Field on Memorial Day. It had been raining almost every day for three weeks. Much preparation had been made for this great service as well as much money spent for advertising, etc.

A special 24-hour prayer meeting was called to pray for the rain to stop and for God's blessings on the proposed meeting to be held the next day. Dr. Johnson asked me to take charge of the prayer time, and many other ministers and church groups participated in this time of prayer. While we prayed in the hotel, we could hear the rain. Just two hours before the 24-hour prayer meeting was over, while many were still praying, I said, "Let us stop asking the Lord to stop the rain and thank Him that there will be no rain tomorrow. We have been asking, now let us believe it and thank God." It was naturally hard to do when the rain was still pouring down. But we did, and the next morning the rain had stopped and the sun was brightly shining.

It was a great day which we shall never forget. The weather reports predicted showers, but there were no showers. During the day, there was rain for five miles all around Chicago, but not in Chicago. There, the sun was shining. Over 65,000 were present at Soldier Field that night to hear the great singing, testimonies and the Gospel preached. Hundreds of people came forward to make decisions for the Lord. This was a great victory. How we praised God! He heard our prayers and the rain was stopped. The next day it rained again and continued every day for an entire week. God moves when we pray.

GOD ANSWERS PRAYER

As I look back upon my own Christian life, I am reminded of a few experiences out of the many hundreds of prayers that God has answered so definitely. Soon after I accepted the Lord Jesus Christ as my Savior, after listening to the pastor challenge us to be soul winners, I began to specifically pray that God would lead me to some lost souls. I shall never forget one Sunday afternoon, after I had spent some time in prayer, I decided to go to Lincoln Park near Moody Church and invite a few sailors to the meeting. Even though I had difficulty with the English language since I had come over from Russia only a few years before, I was able to make contact with nine sailors and explain the way of salvation to them as best I could. They were all grateful to me for speaking to them. I invited them to go with me to the evening service at Moody Church. During the service, I specifically prayed for their souls — and every one of them raised his hand for salvation. I took them to the inquiry room where a personal worker helped them from the Word of God and explained the way of salvation. One of the greatest joys in this world is to point someone to Christ.

One summer soon after my conversion, I was working at Cedar Lake, Indiana, at the Moody Bible Conference. On a Sunday afternoon, as I was by the lake, I began talking to two young men. They were on their way to a dance club across the lake, but I told them that if they were seeking real joy they could find it in Christ. These two young fellows refused to go with me to the Gospel service, but I promised them that I would pray for them while they went to the dance, that the Lord would speak to their hearts. I told them in parting that whenever they felt their need to be saved they should come to the camp and ask for Peter, the Russian, and I would be glad to see them and help them. So they went to the dance and I went to the Bible camp.

I asked another man to join with me and agree together (as the Bible says, "If two of you agree . . .") to pray for these two men who went to the dance club, that God would convict them of their sins and give them no rest until they found Christ as Savior. We spent about an hour in prayer, believing God and trusting Him to work in their hearts.

About two hours later, these two men left the dance club and came to the camp grounds looking for me. At first I did not recognize them and they said, "We are the two fellows you spoke to a few hours ago at the lake and asked if we wanted to be saved. Will you please pray for us?" I gladly took them to the special prayer room and led them both to the Lord Jesus Christ. I asked them why they came so soon from the dance club. They said that when they got there they were so miserable, had misunderstandings with some of their friends, and got so disgusted that they quit the whole thing and came over. Thank God! They were marvelously saved. All three of us began thanking God that He heard our prayers. They went home rejoicing. I saw them from time to time during the summer months, praising the Lord.

There was a Russian young man in Chicago for whom I earnestly prayed. He was leaning toward atheism and laughed at me because I attended church. I told him that I would not stop praying for him until God saved his soul. This man told me that neither I nor God would ever do anything for him because he did not believe in God. But I told him that he would find out in eternity that there is a God — after it was too late — if he did not get right with Him now.

After praying for this man for over a year, one day while I was working I was especially burdened to pray for him. I asked my boss if he would release me early from work because I was under such a terrific burden to pray for this man. He did, and I called on a friend of mine who was a real prayer warrior to pray with me. We spent about two hours in urgent, earnest prayer for the salvation of this young man. It is wonderful to know someone who really loves to pray. You do not have to know how to pray beautiful prayers, the Holy Spirit will pray through you if you will only take time to pray.

The next morning I went to the store where this young man was working. When he saw me coming, he was overjoyed. He said, "Peter, I'm so glad you came to see me. Yesterday I had no rest and I thought I would die. I didn't know what to do with myself. I felt miserable." I said to him, "Praise the Lord. We were praying for you last night." He asked me to please stop praying for him and he would do whatever I told him to do. So I told him that he must give his heart to the Lord and if he did not I would continue to pray for him. He said that he would and promised that the next day, which was Sunday, he would be at the young men's Bible class at Moody Church.

The next afternoon, he was there. When the Bible teacher gave the invitation for salvation, this young fellow walked forward, knelt at the altar and wept, giving his heart to the Lord. After that experience, he told me how he had spiritually suffered in his heart. Though he had previously told me he was happy and satisfied, he never really was. The Lord had heard my prayer. Now I could pray that God would help him to grow in grace. Today that young man is married, has a family, and is rejoicing in the Lord because we took time to pray for him. Keep on praying for your unsaved friends.

After consecrating my life for the Lord's service at a missionary conference at Moody Church, I had a great desire to enter Bible school. For a while, I went to evening classes at Moody Bible Institute. I later graduated from St. Paul Bible Institute in St. Paul, Minnesota. God supplied all my needs in a wonderful way while I was in Bible school, but that is not all. While I was in school, struggling with the English language and my studies, I prayed that God would help me lead many souls to Jesus Christ. This always blessed my soul and kept me from getting discouraged.

During free periods and in the evenings, I always prayed that God would help me to be able to speak to at least one person every day and, if possible, lead him to Christ. One day while I was studying and praying, the Lord put it on my heart to take some Gospel tracts and go for a walk on University Avenue in St. Paul, Minnesota.

I gave out my first tract to a Frenchman who came toward me with a piece of paper in his hand. He asked me to show him the way to the factory named on the paper. I told him I did not know the way to the factory, but I could show him the way to heaven. This man looked at me with a strange expression and said, "Heaven?" I said, "Yes, heaven. After I point out to you the way to heaven, then we shall look for the factory." He agreed.

I showed this man the way of salvation from the Bible and he said that he would like to be saved. We found a church a few blocks away, but the doors were locked. However, since there was an open window, we crawled through the window, went down to the altar in the front of the auditorium, and there we knelt and he gave his heart to the Lord. We thanked God that He had heard our prayers, then went out rejoicing and found the factory he was seeking.

Since Jesus said that He is the way to heaven, we are glad that we can point people to heaven. Yes, God leads as we pray. As you pray for wisdom, I believe He will guide you to the one to whom you should speak.

On another occasion, after prayer, I went to Minneapolis with some Gospel tracts. After walking around and looking over the people, I saw a man in overalls standing against a wall. I went up to him, excused myself, and asked him if he would like to read a tract. I told him I was praying about who to talk to about the Lord and thought I would stop and say hello to him and find out if he was saved. This man said, "How did you know that I am in trouble? I have a wife and two children, yet here I am because I was so drunk my wife asked me to leave home. I am brokenhearted now, not caring so much for my wife, but I love my two precious children. I am without a home and without hope." I told him that there is hope in Christ. Soon this man was in tears, asking who had told me to come and speak to him. I told him it was the Lord. I had prayed to Him about speaking to someone about Christ. He said, "Thank you, friend, for talking to me. I need God's help." Even before I asked him to trust the Lord, he asked me to pray for him.

I took him to a nearby Gospel rescue mission and went to the prayer room where we could have more privacy. We knelt down and I thanked God that He heard my prayer and sent me to help this man. After he cried out to God to forgive him of his sins and save his soul, we got up from our knees. Oh how he thanked me for showing him the way to Christ. He said that he wanted to return to his home, which was about 200 miles from Minneapolis, and tell his family that he was now a different father and a different husband.

A week later, he wrote and thanked me for leading him to a new life in Christ. He said that the first thing he did when he got home was to humble himself and ask his wife and children to forgive him for the way he had lived. He said that now they were a happy family, going to church, and reading the Bible together. From time to time I heard from this man, and he told me how his wife and children also accepted the Lord as Savior and were now living a new and wonderful life in Christ.

It pays to pray that God will lead and guide you to speak to some poor, lost soul about Christ. The Bible says, "If any of you lacks wisdom, let him ask of God, who gives to all liberally and without reproach, and it will be given to him" (James 1:5). We certainly need to ask God for wisdom and guidance in our daily walk and in our witnessing for Him. God hears us and helps us as we come to Him in prayer and trust Him for His leading.

Once I was holding special meetings in Billings, Montana,

and after a service expressed the desire that I would like to go back to Russia to do missionary work, see my parents and tell them about the Lord, whenever the Lord provided the means for such a trip. Two years later, in August 1925, I began to pray and by faith decided to return to Belarus, where I had been born the first time. Just three days after I had made this definite decision to return to Eastern Europe, I received a special delivery letter from a lady who had met me two years before in Billings. She said, "The Lord has laid it on my heart to send you this check for $315. This might help you to get back to Eastern Europe whenever you decide to go." This dear saint did not know that I had already decided to return just three days before that letter arrived, and that hers was the first gift toward my first missionary trip to Russia. By September 17, 1925, the Lord had supplied all my needs, and on October 1, I was on my way. Oh how God worked and definitely answered prayer! He is faithful. Paul said, "And my God shall supply all your need according to His riches in glory by Christ Jesus" (Philippians 4:19). Not our wants, but our needs. I know God answers prayer. I have experienced it and believe it without any doubts.

In 1933, when I was again visiting Belarus and Poland, I also went to Sweden at the invitation of some Christian friends. There, I had the honor of meeting the prince of Sweden in Stockholm. He spoke English and asked me about the work among Russian-speaking people. I told him how God was blessing the work at that time along the borders of Russia. He then told me something which I shall never forget. The prince challenged my heart as he said, "We Scandinavian Christians failed God by not taking the Gospel of Christ into Russia a long time ago. We sent out missionaries into many other parts of the world, but not into Russia. So now we are trying to do all we can to help the Russian people get the Word of God whenever we find the door open."

With that challenge, I began to pray in a new and greater

way concerning the evangelization of the Russian people. I became increasingly burdened for them. With this burden on my heart and mind, I returned to the United States in November of 1933. At that time, I was working with the great evangelist, the late Paul Rader, in his missionary department. However, Paul became ill and strongly advised me to organize a committee for evangelizing the Russian-speaking people. He said that he would probably not be able to help me much any more. He mentioned several outstanding Christian leaders and businessmen in Chicago who might be able to help me start such an organization.

As I thought these things over, I trembled and was much afraid, humanly speaking. But Mr. Rader said to me, "If you only pray, as you have been doing up to this time, God will help you." Several other great Christian leaders from other organizations gave me the same advice and urged me to launch out with a committee to evangelize the Russian-speaking people around the world.

I began to fast and pray, together with my wife, seeking God's leading in this respect and looking for His perfect will in the matter. God gave me a wonderful prayer warrior in the person of my wife, and we spent much time together before the Lord during those important days of decision. There was no doubt as to what my general desire and intentions were for the Lord. He gave me a terrific burden to reach the unreached for Christ. I cried out to God often to help me reach people with the Gospel. He gave me a vision and burden for the lost world. But now as I was crying out to God concerning reaching the Russian people in particular, I felt the Lord's leading to go forward in faith with prayer.

In January 1934, with the help of several Christian businessmen and pastors, the Russian Gospel Association was organized. The name was later changed to Slavic Gospel Association. By prayer and faith we launched out, announcing the members of our committee and the purpose of our work. The hand of God was upon us from the beginning and there was no doubt that the Lord was in it. Three days after the announcement of the new association, we received our first missionary gift. It was a check for nearly $1,000 from some friends whom I had met four years before. The Lord surely works when we trust Him. It is one thing to have faith and to pray, and it is another thing to put our faith into action with some works. "Faith without works is dead." We must pray, believe, and then act. God blessed us for stepping out in faith.

Missionary work is entirely of faith. It is supported by God's children through their freewill offerings and individual gifts. We started this association with the promise to God to begin each day's work with prayer, as well as taking one day each month for prayer and fasting. Because of this, we can see the power of God working in the overruling of oppositions and enemies, opening closed doors, and giving us many victories. We give Him all the glory, praise and honor.

Because God answers prayer, He has opened doors for us to work and preach the Gospel in countries around the world. Scores and scores of souls are being won for the Lord, thousands hear the Gospel who otherwise would never have heard. Much clothing and food have been sent to poor Christians.

ANSWERED PRAYER DURING MISSION TRIPS

Many people ask me how I am financially able to travel and visit the mission fields of the world. Some have even asked if it would not be better to spend the money for poor and needy people in these places. God works in wonderful ways to carry on His work. Since it has been in God's will, He has led me to make these various missionary journeys for the purpose of evangelism, surveying needy fields, conducting Bible conferences and prayer meetings, encouraging missionaries, etc.

If I had never gone to these various mission fields, I would never have received the money used for these trips. God supplied these funds through people who designated their gifts specifically for this purpose. One time I had been praying privately, not mentioning to anyone, that if it was God's will for me to visit war-torn Europe, He would make it possible by supplying my needs. Two Christian friends came to me and said that if the Lord should lead me to go to Eastern Europe, they would like to have a part in helping me with the expense of my trip. I bowed my head and said in my heart, "Thank You, Lord, for answering my prayer."

After I made that trip to Germany, Poland and other countries, and saw the marvelous blessing of God in the saving of many souls, a Christian friend read my report about the trip and said that if I should go back next year to help the poor people in the churches and refugee camps, she would pay for my trip. After I got there, she sent more money to use in the work and to help with the expenses.

In visiting nearly 50 countries around the world with the Gospel since my conversion and dedication to the Lord, God has heard my prayer and laid the burden on the hearts of Christians to help me. In my travels, hundreds have made decisions for Christ and many poor, sick people have received physical and material relief.

In many of the prayer meetings that I have had the joy of conducting, we have seen the wonderful workings of God. One summer at about 4:30 a.m., during an all-night prayer meeting for an upcoming Youth for Christ Congress on Evangelism to be held in Tokyo, a Canadian young man cried out to God that he was willing to sell his insurance policy and give the money to send me to Tokyo to conduct the prayer meetings at the congress. My heart was greatly touched. A few minutes later, another man who had been kneeling by me in prayer put his hand on my shoulder and asked me, "Will you go? I will also help you with your expenses if you go to Tokyo." I felt so unworthy of all these blessings. God's presence was so real in that meeting. However, because our association was in great financial need and I was already booked to speak at nine different Bible conferences that summer, I felt that I must stay by the work at home instead of going to Japan.

I've shared this story to show how God's will must be the main thing in our lives — not money or anything else. His will must be first. Since I was not led of the Lord to go to Japan, those gifts were not given to me. Instead, I fulfilled my engagements at the nine Bible conferences in the United States — and it was one of the most blessed summers I have ever had in the Lord's work. He worked wonderfully. Not only did He bless with many souls saved and hundreds of dedications, but all of the money which was needed by SGA for its worldwide work came in. Oh, how God can bless you and fill you with His grace and Holy Spirit in a new way as you spend time before Him in prayer.

In all of my life I have always sought His will for me, so I have always prayed much before making any decision. I seek only His will. It does not matter whether people understand or not, as long as God understands my heart and directs my paths. God's way is the best way. I want to be a man of prayer, a soul winner and a blessing. I want to be a humble servant of God and do His will. Where He leads me, I will follow.

PIONEER WORK

While I was a student at St. Paul Bible Institute, I prayed much together with my fellow students that God would lead us to be used by Him in places that needed the Gospel. I am glad that God taught us to launch out to work for Him on the streets, in schoolhouses, prisons, hospitals and wherever we had a chance to witness for Him. This was the way I started my ministry for the Lord. As we prayed, He led.

One summer, two other fellows from St. Paul Bible Institute and I visited a town in South Dakota where we did not know a single person and where there was a great need for the Gospel. Since we had prayed much for the Lord's guidance in this matter and since we saw the great need for His message in this town, we decided to start services in this community. Even though we did not have any money with us to carry on any kind of extensive work, we trusted the Lord to supply our needs. We rented a hall right on the main street of town and began evangelistic meetings. The only place for us to sleep was on the floor in the hall. We slept there for two nights. We did not have much to eat, but all of these things drove us to much fasting and prayer with the realization that in our own strength we would accomplish nothing in this place. We believed God would help us and make us a blessing. We had street meetings every day in addition to our evening services. Soon people began to come to our meetings and get saved.

As we stayed on in this town through the summer — praying and trusting God much — our needs were supplied, many souls were saved, Christians were strengthened, and we had a marvelous time. The lesson I learned from our work in this town was not to run away from hard places, but to pray much, trust the Lord to help in every way, and to stick it out.

In those days we went out by faith and in prayer, trusting God to supply our needs, which He did. He is able to do the same today for anyone who will pray and trust Him. He will never leave us nor forsake us.

VISITING SOVIET RUSSIA

In 1937, I prayed with my wife and a few Christian friends about visiting the Soviet Union. Even though these were days of many hardships and persecutions for Christians in Russia, I wanted to observe the conditions and see what I could do to help. Most people I talked to about this matter advised me not to go, telling me that if I went I would never get out. Since everyone discouraged me, I decided not to talk to anyone else about it except the Lord. After praying for a few months, I felt confident that He wanted me to go and was further encouraged by the fact that the Lord supplied all the necessary means to make this trip. He also made it possible for me to get a visa for the Soviet Union and the Siberian region, which were very difficult to obtain at that time.

On my way to Russia, I stopped off at a Gospel workers' conference in Warsaw, Poland. Here again, many of the workers advised me not to go and tried to discourage me as others had done in America. My answer in each instance was that God was able to protect me from all evil. One of the men felt extremely sorry for me and the family I had left in America, for he was certain I would never return to them again. I asked him if he would remember me in prayer and ask God to protect me. His answer was, "Yes, but that will not help." That was the kind of encouragement I received before I entered Russia. But thank God, no harm can be done to those who are in His will, for "if God be for us, who can be against us?"

From Warsaw, I took the train to Kiev, Ukraine. I prayed that God would help me find a Russian Gospel-preaching church. I searched Sunday morning and did not find one, but I was told where the church was located. "If you want to get a seat, you had better get there by 6:00 or 6:30 p.m. because the meeting begins at 7:00." I thought if I arrived 15 minutes before the meeting was scheduled, I would have enough time to get a seat.

Arriving in good time, to my great surprise I found this large church was already overcrowded. Many people were standing in the church and even outside. My heart was thrilled. I could only weep for joy to realize that these dear people were so hungry to hear the Word of God. The meeting opened at exactly 7:00 and several preachers took part in the service.

One of the preachers said, "Dear brothers and sisters, let us thank God for this wonderful opportunity we have to get together once more to worship our Lord Jesus Christ. He is worthy of praise. Let us pray." As soon as the preacher in this evangelical Baptist church announced prayer, people began to pray everywhere. After a long time of prayer, the meeting continued. God's presence was felt. How easily and diligently people pray when they have difficulties. What a challenge this should be to us to have this kind of prayer life no matter what our circumstances of life. God always works when we pray.

As I went on to visit Leningrad (St. Petersburg), I again noticed the great sincerity in the prayer life of Russian Christians. As I stepped inside their church, I found over 500 people kneeling in prayer, both young and old. How my heart was touched to see the children of God not ashamed nor afraid to kneel and pray. I could hardly believe I was in Russia. This prayer meeting reminded me of the weekday prayer meetings at Moody Church in Chicago, where hundreds gathered for prayer. As I knelt in prayer with these dear Christians who endured many hardships for the Gospel's sake, my heart melted. How I thank God for the privilege I had of fellowshipping with them and hearing their wonderful reports of how God was working there among them.

We can understand why Christianity is going forward today in Russia, why many people have a hunger for God as never before, and why there is a spiritual awakening in different parts of Russia. The Russian Christians know how to pray!

When leaving Russia on my way to Japan, I praised God for hearing my prayers while I was in Russia. God was with me. Going through customs, our baggage was examined. Everything was satisfactory. My passport was stamped, and I left. In one hour, the train passed from Russia into Manchuria. My heart was filled with joy and gratitude to God for His complete power and protection. What a joy it is to travel with the Lord.

PRAYING IN JESUS' NAME

Have you ever heard anyone pray and then just stop without asking the request in Jesus' name? I always feel that the prayer is not finished, just like a letter without a signature.

Christ said to those who would take time to talk to God: "And whatever you ask in My name, that I will do, that the Father may be glorified in the Son. If you ask anything in My name, I will do it" (John 14:13-14). It is our privilege to ask, and God has promised to answer. In this promise, there is the condition that we must ask in Jesus' name. We are to pray in Jesus' name — the name of the Son of God. When we do this, we acknowledge the fact that we are praying for His glory and honor and only He has the power and authority to grant our requests. Therefore, when we come to the end of our prayer, it is a good thing to ask everything in Jesus' name. If we do our part, He will do His part.

In Acts 3:6-7, we find that a lame man was seeking help from Peter: "Then Peter said, 'Silver and gold I do not have, but what I do have I give you: In the name of Jesus Christ of Nazareth, rise up and walk.' And he took him by the right hand and lifted him up, and immediately his feet and ankle bones received strength." Yes, this man was healed, but not because of anything Peter could do. Peter came in the name and authority of Jesus to give help in this time of need. We too will receive help in answer to our prayers as we realize that help will only come in the authority and power of Jesus' name. Jesus said, "Until now you have asked nothing in My name. Ask, and you will receive, that your joy may be full" (John 16:24). Fullness of joy and help in time of need can be had in Jesus' name. God wants us to realize that only in and through Him can these things be ours.

A SEMINARY STUDENT WHO COULD NOT PRAY

In my travels in missionary and evangelistic conferences throughout North America and other parts of the world, I meet many students from Bible institutes, colleges and seminaries who come to me and ask questions about their prayer life. One young man was a seminary student who asked, "Mr. Deyneka, what is wrong with my praying? Here I am, dedicated to the Lord, wanting to do God's will, but somehow I just cannot pray. When I go to pray, my mind gets so full of evil thoughts that I just cannot pray. I also have a hard time keeping awake when

I pray and often fall asleep. My mind just fills up with everything except prayer." I am sure that there are hundreds of others with similar problems.

I asked him, "How do you pray and where do you pray?" "Well," he said, "I pray in my bedroom before I go to bed." I asked him, "Do you pray just in your mind or do you pray aloud?" He said, "No, I never pray aloud; I just pray in my mind." I told him that might be his trouble. If he cannot get victory praying silently, he should start praying aloud. Of course God hears us when we pray silently. There is a time and a place for that kind of prayer. But if we are bothered by wandering thoughts and sleepiness when we pray, it helps to pray aloud.

So when you go to pray, pour out your heart before God, claim His promises, claim the victory, ask God to cleanse your heart, mind and even your thoughts. When David prayed he said, "Search me, O God, and know my heart; try me, and know my anxieties" (Psalms 139:23). He not only asked God to search his heart, but also to search his thoughts. So I told this young man that he should search his heart and mind and pray aloud. Since then he has told me that now when he goes to pray, he has victory and does not go to sleep. He opens his heart and mouth and talks to God just as if he were talking to a friend. His heart and mind are clear now, and he is happy and full of the joy of the Lord.

If we meet God's conditions when we come to pray, He has promised to do His part. Our part is to come to Him, to seek Him, to ask of Him in faith and sincerity with a pure heart, to ask in His name and authority, and He will hear and answer our prayers. Do you love the Lord? Then take time to talk to Him. Our prayer of faith will accomplish great things.

4

HOW TO CONDUCT PRAYER MEETINGS

In my travels among various Christian groups, I have often been asked how to conduct prayer meetings. Particularly young people have asked this question because they have wanted to get together with other young people to pray. There are several types of prayer meetings that are commonly held, but all types of prayer meetings are important and all have their place.

PRAYING ALONE

This is the most important of all prayer meetings. A person should never wait until he gets to a church or a prayer meeting to pray. We should pray alone. We should be anxious to talk to our Heavenly Father not just once a day, but many times. Daniel prayed at least three times a day. Paul tells us to pray without ceasing. While we should be in an attitude of prayer throughout the day and pray in the spirit, we should also take time out of our busy day in order to spend it alone with God.

When once asked what were his plans for the following day, Martin Luther answered, "Work, work, work — from early morning until late at night. In fact, I have so much to do that I shall have to spend the first three hours in prayer." The Bible tells us that as we take time to pray in private to God, He will bless. Jesus said, "But you, when you pray, go into your room, and when you have shut your door, pray to your Father who is in the secret place; and your Father who sees in secret will reward you openly" (Matthew 6:6). This is a great promise and challenge for us to pray individually. This verse tells us to get alone somewhere and pray. After we pray secretly, God will reward us openly. As we spend time alone with Jesus, we will become more like Him. People will see a change in our lives. When people saw Peter and John, they knew that these two men had been with Jesus because they were more like Him.

There are many Christians who must always pray alone because there is no one else with whom they can pray. This is the case with some missionaries and Christians in lonely places. The first time I returned to my home in Belarus, I was the only Christian in the village where I was born. For nearly a year, while I was in that area, I had no one with whom to pray. My mother and brother were greatly opposed to me because I was a believer, and they tried to do everything they could to discourage me. When I would sit down to eat and ask the blessing on the meal, they would interrupt my prayer. I had to go out alone with a heavy heart and find some other place to pray. However, I continued to trust the Lord and pray for their salvation even though it seemed like an impossible situation.

On a number of occasions, when returning home late at night after preaching in the surrounding villages, I would stand outside in the cold blizzards of winter and knock on my door — only to be refused entrance because I had been out preaching. All I could do was pray. How I wished that I had someone with whom I could pray and share my burden! How grateful I was, however, for the privilege of coming to the Lord with my burdens and casting them all upon Him. He gave me strength to continue living a testimony before Him, praying for my loved ones. When I was leaving my village to return to the States, my mother was still so opposed to me that she told me never to return home again.

I never gave up praying for my loved ones. Many was the hour that I spent in private intercession on their behalf. Praise God, He heard my prayers! Although I prayed much in private for them, He openly rewarded me and I saw both my mother and brother accept Christ as their personal Savior.

Maybe you are also facing opposition. Maybe people do not want to hear your prayers. Then get alone and pray much to God in secret. He will lift your burdens and give you strength. I have known many people who were persecuted in Eastern Europe and in other places who had to pray alone and in secret. My wife was also opposed by her parents when she accepted Christ as Savior and had to do much praying alone since there were no other Christians in her village to join her.

If you are having experiences similar to those mentioned and have no one to join you and encourage you in prayer, get alone with God. He will encourage you. I want to remind you again that Christ left the crowds, and even His friends, to go to the hillside and pray alone. Often when we walk with Christ, we will have to walk alone on this earth. However, He is always with us, always understands us, and always wants to help us.

SMALL PRAYER MEETINGS

God meets with small groups as well as large. The Scripture talks about small prayer groups and we need not be discouraged when only a few gather to pray. Many have said to me, "But there are just two or three of us who are Christians in the whole house or community." Or others say that there are just a few in the church who are spiritually minded and desire to seek God. Matthew 18:19-20 says, "Again I say to you that if two of you agree on earth concerning anything that they ask, it will be done for them by My Father in heaven. For where two or three are gathered together in My name, I am there in the midst of them." If only two or three meet together and agree in prayer, He will hear and bless.

Probably the most important small group prayer meeting is the family altar. Every Christian home should have a family altar. Even if all of the members of the family are not Christians, those who are believers should unite daily in prayer, remembering those who are not. There is nothing that will hold a family together and bring about spiritual harmony and unity more than family prayer. Times of prayer at the family altar should be informal. The Word of God should be read, the problems of the day discussed, and requests for prayer mentioned. Everyone in the family should pray.

Many Christians meet discouragements and feel they have been forgotten. This is the time to get together with someone else and pray. When Paul and Silas prayed, their chains fell off and they were set free. When you pray, it will change you and your surroundings as well.

I have heard of many clergymen and other believers in Russia who were sent to Siberian prisons because of their faith. Yet even there they found other believers with whom they prayed. God did wonders for them, heard their prayers, and kept them encouraged while going through suffering for the Gospel.

CHURCH PRAYER MEETINGS

In Acts 3:1 we read, "Now Peter and John went up together to the temple at the hour of prayer, the ninth hour." Notice that Peter and John went to the temple to pray. They had a specific time and place when they gathered for prayer. We know that the church where we worship together in song and sermon is also a place where we should meet for prayer. Jesus said that His house shall be called a house of prayer. Therefore it is God's will that we, as Christians, should meet together with other Christians in a church for prayer.

If a church does not have a regular prayer meeting it cannot prosper and grow spiritually, because prayer is the power behind the program of the church. Even as machinery does not work well without oil, the activities of the church will not go forward as they should without the oil of the Holy Spirit which comes through prayer. As Christians come together to pray, it is a time for praise to God, confession of sins, renewing of fellowship, intercession for others, and another opportunity for believers to be reminded of their need for total dependence upon God for any success in the church program. The unity of Christians in prayer brings down God's power upon a church.

I have noticed in my travels that the praying church is the growing church. You will always find it that way. It is not only a growing church, but it is a going church. The praying church is doing something for God. It is a missionary-minded church. In this type of church we find people praying for one another, their pastor, their Sunday school teachers and pupils, their missionaries, and anyone else connected with their church. They are praying for revival in their church and for God's blessings on all the activities of their church program. As a rule, you will find that the more spiritually minded people are the ones who come out to the weekday prayer meetings, because they love the Lord and want to continue to see His blessings upon their own lives and in the life of their church.

Shortly after my conversion at Moody Church in Chicago, I began to attend their prayer meetings. At first I was very much afraid to pray in public because I was a new convert and because of my difficulty with the English language. But as I came to the prayer meetings and heard others pray, I was inspired. Having a hunger to know more about God, I also began to pray publicly. What a great blessing that was in my life! From that time on, I never wanted to miss the prayer meetings.

I often came to prayer meeting a little bit downhearted because of my circumstances as a new immigrant in America. But after hearing the singing, testifying and praying, I would pray and be greatly uplifted in my soul. All of my discouragements fled. I began to urge my friends to come and experience the same thing that I had experienced.

There are many ways that church prayer meetings may be conducted. They usually begin with a period of singing. This is good for the heart and a time of real blessing. The songs are often followed by a time of testimonies, when Christians can glorify the Lord by thanking Him for what He has done for them during the week. This is a source of encouragement to other Christians. After this, many pastors give a brief message from God's Word. The length of the message should allow time for everyone who would like to pray to take part. Since this is a prayer meeting, one should spend as much time as possible in prayer. Prayer requests should be given by the pastor and the congregation just before the prayer time.

HOME PRAYER MEETINGS

In Acts 12:11-12 we read, "And when Peter had come to himself, he said, 'Now I know for certain that the Lord has sent His angel, and has delivered me from the hand of Herod and from all the expectation of the Jewish people.' So, when he had considered this, he came to the house of Mary, the mother of John whose surname was Mark, where many were gathered together praying." There are many times when Christians will want to meet together in homes to pray for special requests. Sometimes people are unable to get out to the church prayer meeting, or there might not be a church nearby. Other times believers just feel led to gather together in homes. This was the case in the early church during the time Peter was put in jail.

During times of testing in Russia, many Christians met in homes for prayer. A man in Russia once told me there were thousands of Russian Christians praying together in homes in order to help them stand in the midst of trials. In fact, there were many more praying in homes than in churches. As a result, the Russian Christians have stood strong for the Lord and God is doing a new thing among them these days.

Home prayer meetings may be held any time it is convenient. Often a group of women may gather during the day to pray for their friends who need Christ or for some special need of the church. Women's missionary prayer groups also meet in the morning or afternoon to remember the needs of their missionaries. Young people's groups and Sunday school classes might meet in the evening during the week to pray for the unsaved in their midst and for guidance in the future.

I knew of a group of young people who gathered in a home every Monday night from different churches in a large city to pray for special youth activities and missionary work. God hears us wherever we are. If we take time to talk to Him, He will do for us more than we expect — just as the people experienced as they prayed for Peter and saw him released from jail.

Home prayer meetings may be simple and informal. After the group gathers, a hymn or chorus may be sung from memory, a few verses of Scripture read or some promises of God quoted, and then prayer requests given and discussed. There need not be many preliminary matters. The emphasis should be on prayer. These times of prayer fellowship together will be refreshing and rewarding.

UNITED PRAYER MEETINGS

This is an important type of prayer meeting. There are times when we should not only have prayer meetings conducted by single groups or churches, but by many groups and churches coming together for united prayer. Acts 4:31 says, "And when they had prayed, the place where they were assembled together was shaken; and they were all filled with the Holy Spirit, and they spoke the word of God with boldness."

We have many such prayer meetings throughout North America and other parts of the world among different Christian groups. For example, Christian businessmen in various cities unite to pray for revival and special projects which they promote to win people to Christ. Youth for Christ unites Christian workers at various rallies and conferences each year to pray for teen-agers, missionary work, revival and salvation of souls around the world.

Churches in some cities have weekly or monthly united prayer meetings at which time many people fast and pray for revival and the salvation of souls in their city. We have had such meetings in Chicago for many years. I have found that through united prayer meetings, new unity comes about and a new fellowship is established among Christians.

Some years ago, I was in an area in Poland where there were a few Christians living in scattered villages but no Gospel-preaching churches had yet been established. We called many of these Christians together and started prayer meetings among them. As a result of these united prayer meetings, the people became challenged and inspired — so much so that they went out and started Gospel work where nothing had been done before and a new church was established. As we come together to pray for definite requests, God will lead us out into action.

ALL-NIGHT PRAYER MEETINGS

This is perhaps the hardest kind of prayer meeting. After praying for several hours into the night, we tend to get weary. Yet there is a definite place and need for extended periods of prayer. When we call an all-night prayer meeting, we have a special purpose in mind. We aim at something definite and urgent — spiritual awakening, conviction of sinners, spiritual hunger among Christians for revival. When we attend these prayer meetings, we do so because we really mean business with God and have urgent burdens on our hearts that we want God to meet. Great victories have been won through prayer during the night hours.

During the Youth for Christ World Congress on Evangelism held in Belfast, Ireland, after we made an announcement that we were going to have an all-night prayer meeting, a Christian leader asked, "What can you pray about all night?" I am sure that many other Christians also have this question in mind and even smile at the announcement of an all-night prayer meeting. Some say, "Why pray all night? The day is long enough." Well, these people forget or do not realize that we can pray day and night and still never "finish" praying. There are scores of things to pray about if we will just take time to meet with God.

When we take the time, as we do at these prayer meetings, we can pray about everything that is on our heart. That night of prayer in Belfast was one of the best I have ever attended. Many Christian leaders and laymen were revived and received a new vision of what could be done for the Lord. God met us in an especially powerful way.

In conducting all-night prayer meetings (I have been in hundreds of such prayer meetings and God has given me the privilege of leading many of them), we organize the time of prayer in accordance with the requests. We do not just pray around the world in a general way all night. The prayer leader explains to the people the order in which the requests are to be handled so the people can be praying in agreement. Of course, the Holy Spirit leads us to pray for other things even though we might be thinking of certain requests, but we try to emphasize particular requests at a particular time. As the night wears on, we take new requests as the Lord leads. This way we can pray about many things in unity, and from hour to hour the people know what they are to pray for.

During the course of the night, we try to change our positions about every hour. During these breaks, we have the people stand up, sing a song, and maybe have a few testimonies. Then just before we resume prayer again, someone shares an 8-10 minute challenge from the Bible on prayer, faith, the victorious life, or some other promise of God. We do not try to preach a sermon during this time, but just give an inspiring exhortation to help the people in their prayer life. This will also be a time when the Holy Spirit will search and examine the hearts and lives of the people so they can get right with God.

Of course, breaks in the meeting will depend entirely on the leading of the Holy Spirit. Although we may plan to pray for only a period of one hour, we should continue to pray when the Spirit begins to work and people really get hold of God.

When one prays aloud, he should raise his voice so that all present can hear. It will be an inspiration and blessing to others. We know that God hears us even when we pray quietly, but in prayer meetings such as this, others also want to join in.

When one leads in prayer, we should all be of one spirit. We do not have to be ashamed to say "Amen" if the expression comes from the heart. In this way, we show our agreement and enthusiasm. If a person knows that God the Holy Spirit is blessing his soul, it is wonderful when an expression of agreement and enthusiasm comes right from his heart.

I heard a story once about a man who always said "Amen" and "Praise the Lord." One Sunday the pastor announced that they would have a visiting speaker next Sunday. The pastor privately asked this man if he would kindly be quiet when the visitor spoke. He told him, "If you be quiet and do not say 'Amen' or 'Praise the Lord,' I will give you a pair of boots." The man was in desperate need of a pair of boots, so he agreed. The next Sunday morning, when the speaker began preaching about the second coming of our Lord, this man could not be quiet. His heart was so blessed that he shouted, "Praise the Lord! Boots or no boots!"

Concerning the schedule during these nights of prayer, we begin with a searching of our own hearts. David cried out in Psalm 139:23, "Search me, O God, and know my heart; try me, and know my anxieties." We must be willing to confess and repent of our failures, shortcomings, sins and coldness of heart, in order that we might be prepared to pray for other things. Before we pray for someone else, our own hearts must be right with God.

We often have testimonies in the middle and sometimes at the end of the prayer meeting, when people report God's blessing and victory in their hearts. I have heard scores of these testimonies from people who have come with problems and lack of dedication, but after praying they have shared how God spoke to them and met with them in a mighty way. These testimonies are inspiring and challenging to other people. In many of these meetings I have seen people who have come to the night of prayer merely out of curiosity — to see what goes on and how people pray all night — but after they hear the testimonies and see what God has done, the Holy Spirit gets hold of their hearts and they begin to pray and surrender their lives.

During my three years at St. Paul Bible Institute, where we had a night of prayer every Friday, I only missed about six all-night meetings. I did not want to miss them because they were such wonderful and blessed meetings. As we spent time in prayer, we felt we had more spiritual power in our lives and our testimony was more effective. We prayed very specifically that God would help us to be better soul winners and that we might reach many for Christ. Over the past years, I have met some with whom I used to pray at these meetings and have seen that God is using them. I know without any doubt that because of those times of prayer at St. Paul Bible Institute, God changed my life and I am what I am today because there is power and victory in prayer. It was at those prayer meetings that God spoke and led me into full-time Christian service.

When I returned to Chicago from a trip to Europe, I had several nights of prayer with a group of teen-aged boys in our home. God spoke to them, and today they are leaders in Christian service being greatly used of God.

During my two visits to SGA's Russian Bible school in Argentina, we had all-night prayer meetings. The students had never experienced anything like it before. Many of them said afterward that they never really knew what prayer was. Those meetings revolutionized many of their lives. They received a new vision and burden. One of the students was so moved, challenged and changed by the Holy Spirit during that night of prayer that he spent the next night returning by train to the place where he was doing missionary work — tired and weary, but full of the joy of the Lord. He immediately went to the home of an unsaved man and told him about the living Christ. After being shown from the Word of God about the Lord, the man broke down and wept and received Christ as his Savior.

The length of the night of prayer will depend on the leading of the Holy Spirit. As the people pray, they will feel that victory has been reached in their own lives and burdens lifted. Then it is time to praise God for what He has done.

ENCOURAGING INDIVIDUALS TO PRAY

How can you get others to pray? When you stand before a group of people at a prayer meeting, let them see from God's Word why they must pray. Jude says in verse 20-21, "But you, beloved, building yourselves up on your most holy faith, praying in the Holy Spirit, keep yourselves in the love of God, looking for the mercy of our Lord Jesus Christ unto eternal life." God says that the way to be spiritual and the way to build yourself up in the faith is by praying in the Holy Spirit. Therefore, if a Christian wants to grow spiritually and be built up in the faith, he must read the Word of God and have faith while praying. There are many who have been Christians for years but are very weak spiritually. They have no testimony, no victory, no joy, no blessing, and are not winning souls. But they can still build themselves up and experience a different life if they will start to pray.

In prayer meetings, we should encourage individuals to pray claiming the promises of God. In the Bible He shows us His promises and expects us to pray because of what He has promised to do if we pray. Therefore, every Christian can and should be a prayer warrior. New or timid Christians who feel they do not know how to pray should be encouraged to simply ask or thank God concerning various necessities and requests, just as they would talk to one of their friends. In James 4:2 we read, "You do not have because you do not ask." This should be pointed out to those who have never experienced the joy of answered prayer because they have never asked. We must pray if we are to get God's help.

There are many who are afraid to pray publicly. We should

encourage these friends to take part in the prayer meeting, even if it is only briefly. It will bless their hearts and bring victory and encouragement to them. They may be afraid because they cannot pray beautiful prayers like some others, but they should be encouraged to know that this is not necessary with God. He wants everyone to talk to Him like a child would talk to his father or mother.

During one summer while I was in Bible school, I had some meetings in South Dakota. I remember one meeting in a country schoolhouse which was packed with people whom I had never met. Before the meeting that night, I asked someone if they knew any man in the congregation who could lead in prayer during the service. That person told me Mr. Johnson was present, who was a good religious man. When we began the service, I called out and said, "Before I bring the message, I am going to ask Mr. Johnson to lead us in prayer." He shouted back from the audience, "No thank you. You do the praying yourself." I prayed, but after the service he came up to me and apologized. He said that he had never prayed publicly in his life. I encouraged him that if he was born again, he should pray whenever the opportunity presented itself.

A number of years ago, a well-known preacher asked me to come to his church for two weeks and teach his men how to pray. During the day I spoke with the men individually and showed them what it was to pray, and highlighted the necessity and joy of prayer. We called for a men's prayer meeting in the church on Saturday night, and after that first meeting the men continued with the Saturday night prayer meeting for over 20 years. Once they got started, the men learned the joy of prayer fellowship. Everywhere I go I try to encourage people to pray publicly. It encourages and strengthens them as they take part.

WHAT TO PRAY ABOUT

In Philippians 4:6-7 we read, "Be anxious for nothing, but in everything by prayer and supplication, with thanksgiving, let your requests be made known to God; and the peace of God, which surpasses all understanding, will guard your hearts and minds through Christ Jesus." These verses show that we are to take time to pray about anything and everything that concerns us. We are not to worry. We are not to make decisions first and then pray about them later to see if it is God's will. We are not to be careless about our actions. In everything we do, we should pray first, with thanksgiving. When we make all of our requests known to God, He has promised to supply all of our needs according to His riches in glory and to give us peace of heart and mind which passes all understanding. We get real victory and power in our lives when we bring all of our needs and desires to God in prayer.

Praying is not preaching or making a speech to God or to others in our prayer group. We do not pray in order to impress people with our prayers. God wants us to come to Him in simple faith and sincerity with our thanksgiving and requests. We should therefore be specific in our praying.

Hannah said in 1 Samuel 1:27, "For this child I prayed, and the Lord has granted me my petition which I asked of Him." You have specific needs; pray for them. Ask God for exactly what you want Him to do. Hannah's prayer was specific and the Lord gave her the petition which she desired of Him. Have you ever had the experience of asking God for something specific and receiving it from Him?

In 2 Kings 2:9, when Elijah was ready to be caught up into heaven, he told Elisha to ask anything that he wanted God to do for him. Elisha said, "Please let a double portion of your spirit be upon me." He was very specific in what he wanted God to do for him, and God answered his prayer. When Elisha stood before the Jordan River and smote the waters, they parted by the power of God. When the people saw this they said, "The spirit of Elijah rests on Elisha." He went on to perform many other great things in the power and spirit of God. He prayed specifically and to the point. Elisha received what he asked for, to the glory of God. So we must pray to the point and ask God to supply our needs according to His will.

In group prayer meetings, when many requests are made, it is a good thing for individuals to take different requests in order that all of the requests may be brought before the Lord, instead of only a few being repeated by all who pray. One person should not try to take all of the requests. They may either be divided up among the people before going to prayer, or remembered by the people one at a time as they take their turns to pray.

We should specifically pray for those for whom we are concerned about their salvation, "for this is good and acceptable in the sight of God our Savior, who desires all men to be saved and to come to the knowledge of the truth" (1 Timothy 2:3-4). I remember some years ago, during an evangelistic conference held at Moody Church, we had an all-night prayer meeting. During the meeting, a mother with tears in her eyes pleaded that we would pray for her son in order that God would save him, even as soon as the following day at the evangelistic service. This mother was scheduled to speak the following night, so we earnestly prayed that God would convict this man and save him. There was much united prayer for him during that night. At the Saturday night service, after the evangelistic message when the call was given for those who wanted to receive Christ as Savior, this young man — with tears in his eyes — was the first to go forward to give his heart to God. Today, that young man is on fire for the Lord and is preaching the Gospel with great power and blessing. Parents, do not give up praying for your children.

We should not only pray for our family and friends, but also our enemies. Jesus said in Matthew 5:44, "Love your enemies, bless those who curse you, do good to those who hate you, and pray for those who spitefully use you and persecute you."

Prayer requests should also be made for the various Christian workers we know. Even while Paul was in prison, he made the following requests to his Christian friends, "Continue earnestly in prayer, being vigilant in it with thanksgiving; meanwhile praying also for us, that God would open to us a door for the Word, to speak the mystery of Christ, for which I am also in chains" (Colossians 4:2-3). Even though he was in chains, spiritually he was enjoying full liberty. He asked them to pray for him, that he might have an open door to witness for Christ wherever he was. We should pray for pastors, missionaries and other Christian workers, that they might have the right opportunities and open doors to preach the Gospel.

BIBLE STUDIES IN PRAYER MEETINGS

Bible studies are important and they should prepare the people for prayer, but they should leave enough time so the people can express their needs, desires and requests in prayer. Hebrews 4:12 tells us, "For the Word of God is living and powerful, and sharper than any two-edged sword, piercing even to the division of soul and spirit, and of joints and marrow, and is a discerner of the thoughts and intents of the heart." Bible studies should reveal the needs of the people and give them a hunger and desire for a closer walk with God. Only the Word of God can challenge us in this way.

LENGTH OF PRAYERS

When we pray privately, we can spend more time on private matters and burdens, praying around the world for all our friends and missionaries with all of their many needs and requests. When Jesus was alone, He prayed much. In fact He prayed all night on occasions. Luke tells us in chapter 6, verse 12, "Now it came to pass in those days that He went out to the mountain to pray, and continued all night in prayer to God." In John 17, we see Jesus praying much for His friends. We should take the example of Christ and pray much in private, bringing before the Lord all of our needs and problems as well as the needs of our friends.

However when praying in united groups, our prayers should be shorter and to the point. The public prayers of Jesus were very short in comparison with His private times of prayer. Many times in prayer meetings someone starts to pray long prayers which are not specific; they are general and tiring.

Wilfred Grenfell, who became a great missionary to Labrador, was a medical student at the time D. L. Moody was preaching in England. Before Grenfell became a Christian, he went for the first time to hear Moody. This is his own account of the service: "It was so new to me that when a tedious prayer time began with a long oration, I started to leave. Suddenly the leader, who afterwards I discovered was D. L. Moody, called out to the audience, 'Let us sing a hymn while our brother finishes his prayer.' His practicality interested me and I stayed through the service." Grenfell was saved shortly thereafter.

If we are in a prayer meeting where there are many others who desire to take part, we must not take all of the time for prayer ourselves. In an all-night prayer meeting, individual prayers should not be too long since each person will have a number of opportunities to pray. Our praying should be specific, to the point, and in the Spirit so that others will also have a chance to pray. Our private prayers can be longer.

CONSECRATION IN PRAYER MEETINGS

In all-night prayer meetings, I have seen many pastors and other Christian workers marvelously dedicate and rededicate their lives to God. The all-night prayer meetings held in Belfast, Ireland, in connection with a Youth for Christ congress were unforgettable. When we started praying one night about 10:00 p.m., the church where the meeting was held was filled with hundreds of praying people. I had never been in such a prayer meeting before. From 10:00 p.m. to nearly 6:00 in the morning, only a few people left the meeting. We felt the presence of God with great power. About 3:00 a.m., many of the British,

American and European workers who were present dedicated their lives to God, being willing to go to other fields as the Lord should lead them. As a result of this prayer meeting, another all-night meeting was called by the British pastors and youth leaders in order to continue praying for a spiritual awakening in Great Britain.

In 1955, it was my privilege to preach to Russian-speaking people in Sao Paulo, Brazil, and also to lead the all-night prayer meeting of the Youth for Christ congress which was held there. Again, we saw the Holy Spirit work in power. The more God's people pray, the more opportunity the Holy Spirit has to work in our hearts and show us our needs. The trouble is that we are often in so much of a hurry and are so busy that we give God little opportunity to speak to us.

At about 4:00 a.m. during this meeting in Sao Paulo, we were going to close, but the Lord laid it on my heart to make one more request. I asked, "Is there anyone here, whether he is a pastor, director, delegate or missionary, who has not yet completely yielded his life to God?" Many responded and came forward to rededicate their lives. Among them was an American pastor from South Bend, Indiana, who came forward and asked to say a few words. He said to the people, "I am a minister. I have a wonderful church in South Bend, but I must confess that the Holy Spirit has spoken to me in this meeting. I have been a pastor without a burden for souls, no love for souls, no love for people. Friends, I want to yield my life completely to God this morning. I would rather die here in South America than go back to my church in the same spiritual condition as when I left." This testimony and broken heart moved upon the hearts of the others there. God began to speak to people, and everywhere they were in tears. We knelt together and prayed for this minister. Oh, how God gave the victory to this brother, and how he thanked God for speaking to him and giving him a new touch from heaven.

After this, others began to come forward, some missionaries, national pastors and evangelists, confessing their needs and asking for prayer. The Lord again performed great wonders through prayer in these Christian workers' lives as they came forward in new surrender and dedication. That minister from Indiana went back to his home church on fire for God, saw a new awakening among the people, and then went out into evangelistic work, preaching on prayer and revival. It pays to pray and wait on the Lord. He renews our strength and gives power to those who pray.

How I thank God for all these years in my life that I have been able to serve Him! How precious and encouraging has been the fellowship in prayer with others. I have often prayed with just one or two, and God has done marvelous things for us. The Lord can do the same for you. Let us mean business with God and take time to pray.

5

VICTORIOUS LIVING THROUGH PRAYER

The reason that many do not or cannot pray through to victory is because there is a hindrance in their lives. These hindrances cause a person to have no peace, joy, rest or confidence even during or after praying. In Isaiah 59:1-2 we read, "Behold, the Lord's hand is not shortened, that it cannot save; nor His ear heavy, that it cannot hear. But your iniquities have separated you from your God; and your sins have hidden His face from you, so that He will not hear." God is telling us very plainly that a great hindrance in the Christian life is sin. These sins are often known hindrances that people are too proud or unwilling to admit, and therefore cause them to miss out on a victorious happy life. God is willing and ready to hear our cries, but sin separates us from Him.

Jesus said that if we pray while having something in our hearts against our brother or sister which we are not willing to forgive, neither will our heavenly Father forgive us our trespasses. As Christians, we have no right and must not hold any evil in our hearts against anyone. We may not agree with other people's actions or opinions, but we must still love them for the sake of their souls. A Christian will not have victory until he asks God for forgiveness. If a Christian is not willing to forgive others, he will harm himself more than anyone else because he will be grieving the Holy Spirit in his own life.

When I was in Bible school, we had special men's prayer

meetings. At one of these meetings one of my fellow students came to me and said, "Brother Deyneka, I want to make a confession to you. For the past year I have held many hard feelings, resentments and jealousies against you and have had no rest in my heart about it. I have suffered greatly. I want you to forgive me." I said, "Yes, you are forgiven, but I didn't know anything about it. This is news to me." This dear man never hurt me, but he did great harm to himself spiritually. How many Christians are there today who are suffering and living defeated lives because of criticism, jealousy and unforgiving attitudes?

Concerning another hindrance, a preacher once told me about a young man who had come to the altar six times, weeping and crying unto God to give him victory in his life. But he always left the altar without victory. He was just the same. All of his prayers and tears did not help him. Why? Because he was not willing to give up something in his life. Finally, when he came forward the seventh time, the preacher put his hand on the young man's shoulder and said, "Young man, what sin do you have in your life that you are not willing to give up?" Immediately this young man cried out, "Lord, you may take Mary out of my life."

This young man was a Christian and he was planning to marry an unsaved girl. In his heart he knew it was the wrong thing to do, but he did not want to give her up. All this while he had no victory or joy. She was a hindrance to victory in his spiritual life. When he was willing to give her up, he received great victory and joy in his heart. This young man told his girlfriend that he could not marry her because she was not born again. She saw that her former friend had something in his life that she did not have.

At one camp where I was speaking for a week, all the young people who were saved came forward to make spiritual dedications of one sort or another. After this happened, all of the unsaved who were present accepted Christ as Savior.

Two of the girls in attendance had stolen some things while on their way to camp. After they came to the meetings and saw Christians getting right with God, they became so convicted of their sin that they could not sleep the entire night. They came forward and got right with God. They went to the camp director and after confessing to him what they had done, they went with him to the store where they had taken the things and confessed to the store manager what they had done. They also told him that they had gotten right with God. The manager forgave them and was impressed with their desire to make things right. At the next meeting in the camp, they gave testimony as to how the Lord had given them great victory.

David said in Psalm 66:18, "If I regard iniquity in my heart, The Lord will not hear." David knew that as long as he had sin in his life, his fellowship with God was not what it should be and his prayers would not be heard and answered.

After the children of Israel had tried to live for God while living in sin at the same time, God said to them, as written in Isaiah 1:15-16, "When you spread out your hands, I will hide My eyes from you; even though you make many prayers, I will not hear. Your hands are full of blood. Wash yourselves, make yourselves clean; put away the evil of your doings from before My eyes. Cease to do evil." God told them the only way their prayers would be heard was if they would quit their lives of sin and disobedience. They could not live in sin and yet try to serve God and have their prayers answered at the same time.

While hindrances greatly hurt the Christian life, a person can be delivered from these sins if he will only repent. Until a person humbles himself and confesses his faults, his iniquities will remain in his heart and he will continue to live a defeated life. Proverbs 15:29 tells us, "The Lord is far from the wicked, but He hears the prayer of the righteous." This is very plain. The reason why many people do not have victory in their lives is because they work and struggle and have problems in their lives which they try to solve in their own strength.

GETTING RIGHT WITH GOD THROUGH PRAYER

We read in God's Word that, "If we confess our sins, He is faithful and just to forgive us our sins and to cleanse us from all unrighteousness" (1 John 1:9). Getting right with God through prayer demands that a condition must be first met, as is seen in the preceding verse. If we come to God in humble prayer and meet the condition by confessing and turning from our sin, God will be faithful to forgive us and cleanse us from all unrighteousness. Thank God that when we come to Him in prayer with our sins, He not only forgives us but also forgets our sins. Through His strength, we are able to live a victorious life.

A woman who was at one of my meetings on the border of Russia represents thousands of similar cases. She had become a Christian some time before, had been baptized, and was a member of a church. At the time I met her, she was not having much fellowship with God or her husband. He was an unsaved man and she always argued with him. She tried to force him to go to church with her, but since she was not a happy or victorious Christian, he did not see any difference between his life and hers and therefore did not see why he should go to church.

When I spoke at the church she attended, I preached about victorious Christian life. She came up to me after the service and said, "Brother Deyneka, I've been a church member for ten years but have no victory in my life. I lose patience with my husband because he will not come to church with me." She asked me how she could get real victory in her life and get her husband to go to church with her. I said the first thing to do was to ask God for forgiveness, and then ask Him for more patience and love for her husband. I told her that she should not preach to her husband, but should spend more time praying for him and above all living a good example of the Christian life.

She said, "How can I win him to Christ if I don't talk to him?" I said, "Just pray for him. He must see a change in your life before he will want Christ as his own Savior. He has heard enough preaching from you. Now he must see more living on your part." In tears, she asked God to forgive her and to help her be a different Christian and a different wife. She also promised to pray for her husband.

For three months after that, she did not say a word about Christ to her husband. Soon the husband noticed that she was a different woman and finally asked her what had happened to her. He wanted to know where she went that made her so different. When she told him, he asked to go to church with her. At the first meeting he attended, he was gloriously saved. As this woman came to God in prayer with her sins, the Lord gave her victory.

There was a woman in another town where I was preaching who was a church member, baptized and active in her church. But she had no joy in her spiritual life or power in her prayers. For many years, her life consisted of only good works. After hearing a message on the victorious Christian life, she came forward and said that not only did she not have victory in her life, but she was not sure she was saved. She was a professing Christian, but did not have anything real in her life. After she prayed and got right with God, she had the assurance of salvation by faith and got victory in her life through prayer.

As a person examines his life and comes to God with humility, God changes that life through prayer so that other lives are reached and God is glorified.

David gave us the right attitude that we are to have in coming to God in order to get right with Him through prayer. He said in Psalm 139:23-24, "Search me, O God, and know my heart; try me, and know my anxieties; and see if there is any wicked way in me, and lead me in the way everlasting." Only as we are willing to lay bare our soul, life, thoughts and all that we are before a holy God and cry out to Him with a sincere prayer for forgiveness and help, will we get right with Him and be what He wants us to be before Him.

Concerning this same matter, Daniel 9:20 says, "Now while I was speaking, praying, and confessing my sin and the sin of my people Israel, and presenting my supplication before the Lord my God . . . " Even Daniel, that great man of God, humbled himself and admitted his need by confessing his sins to God in prayer. Not many people today are willing to confess their sins. If the great men of the Bible needed to confess their needs and faults and get right with God, surely we need to confess what is not right in our lives so we also may have victory.

On one of my trips to South America, I was speaking in a church in Argentina on how to have victory in the Christian life and the importance of prayer in this respect. Two women came to the front after the service and asked for prayer. When I asked them what they wanted me to pray for, they said, "For our unsaved husbands." Before praying for their husbands, I asked them if they were living a Christian life before their husbands in their homes. Both of these Christian women burst into tears. They cried out to God. One started to pray, "It is true, God. I am the one who needs cleansing and forgiveness. I am not living as I should before my husband. Forgive me." The other woman also began to pray for herself. Thank God, both women confessed their sins and got right with God and then started to pray for their husbands in a new way.

In another somewhat similar case, I was speaking in the United States at a Sunday morning service. I was preaching on victory in Christ. We felt the presence of the Lord moving upon the congregation in a wonderful way. As I closed the message, I gave the invitation for any who wanted to raise their hand indicating a desire to get right with God. Many hands were raised, but one woman got up from her seat and came to the front of the auditorium. As she turned to the congregation she said, "As you know, I am the president of the women's prayer group and I have been very active in the church. In fact, I have been so busy, I have had no time to pray. I have also been so busy that I neglected to look after my husband as I should in preparing meals, etc. and have no victory in my own life." She used to tell her husband, "If you are hungry, you know where the store is. Go and buy some food. I am too busy." She said that God convicted her during the message and she asked forgiveness of the people for the way she had been living. She then walked to her husband, threw her arms around him, and publicly asked forgiveness of him. Her husband wept and the entire congregation was moved. With tears, we had a real awakening in the church that morning. The Lord met this woman's spiritual need.

How many people do we have in our churches today who pray for others, seeing faults only in other lives yet never seeing or admitting unconfessed sin in their own hearts and lives? Too many Christians try to cover up sins with good works and try to outweigh evil with good. We know that regardless of how much good we try to do, God still hates sin even though He loves the sinner. Some may think that little sins do not mean very much, but God calls sin sin — no matter how big or small we might think it is. All sin hinders our fellowship with God and defeats our victorious life. All sin must be confessed and forsaken for us to please God. Sin continues to be sin until it is confessed and forsaken.

We read in Galatians 6:7-8, "Do not be deceived, God is not mocked; for whatever a man sows, that he will also reap. For he who sows to his flesh will of the flesh reap corruption, but he who sows to the Spirit will of the Spirit reap everlasting life." Paul warns us not to be deceived. Do not think that God does not see and know what you are doing and the kind of life that you are living. If we are sowing to the flesh and not to the Spirit, we shall reap in the flesh and regret it later on. Many Christians are suffering because they are paying the price for what they have sowed. May the Lord help us to sow in the Spirit, with love and patience. May we remove every hindrance in our lives and may we have a forgiving spirit toward one another, forgiving one another even as Christ has forgiven us. As we do this daily, dying to ourselves and to our surroundings just as Paul said he died daily, we will achieve victory in and through our prayers and live victoriously day by day.

REVIVAL THROUGH PRAYER AND FASTING

God can remove every mountain and every problem if we are only willing to humble ourselves and give ourselves to sincere prayer. I believe that one of the great problems and troubles today among many Christian workers, leaders and church members is that they are not willing to humble themselves and ask God to search their hearts and reveal their needs. Usually when we ask God to send a revival and do a new work in our midst we say, "Lord, we are a needy people, we need a revival." Yes, that is what we need, but it must be a personal thing. Revival must first begin in the individual Christian's heart. The first thing David prayed and asked the Lord was to search his heart and life. We should pray, "Lord, I need a revival, I am the needy one." If every one of us would humble himself and admit to God that "I" need a revival as much as those around us, God would see our humility and sincerity and meet our needs and send revival.

To have a revival does not mean that we have to assemble great crowds and special meetings. God can start revival with anyone anywhere who seeks Him on his face in sincere prayer and honest confession. The Welsh revival began when a few people met in a small place to pray and believe God. The revival spread from their small group to other places. The Lord can do the same thing today in your heart and mine as we meet His conditions. Psalm 85:6 says, "Will You not revive us again, that Your people may rejoice in You?" And Habakkuk 3:2 states, ". . . O Lord, revive Your work in the midst of the years . . ." These were the cries of two men in the Old Testament, and they should be our cry as well.

In many biblical examples, we see that powerful things happened when God's children took the time to fast and pray. In Mark 9:28-29, Jesus told His disciples that a demon in a certain boy could be cast out only through prayer and fasting. And in Acts 13:1-3, as Christians prayed and fasted, God spoke and chose Paul and Barnabas to serve Him in a special way. After Nehemiah cried out to God with much prayer and fasting, as recorded in Nehemiah 1:4, God changed the heart of the king to allow Nehemiah to return to Jerusalem to rebuild the walls of the city. Nehemiah showed his humility and earnestness by fasting. Fasting is important in the right time and place, because it reveals our earnestness before God.

Fasting in and of itself offers no gain or merit before God. Rather, it is the desire to know more of God and get something special from Him that causes us to fast and pray in all earnestness. The way to victory and revival in our churches — if we really mean business with God — is through prayer and fasting. Many Christians set aside a time specifically for this.

There can be no real revival without much prayer. Every Christian worker should spend much time on his knees. In the last several years of my ministry, as I have traveled in many parts of the world where people have spent much time in prayer for spiritual awakening, I have seen great blessings of the Lord as people searched their hearts, confessed their sins before God and even before one another, making things right with others. And God worked! Revival can be ours if we truly desire it.

Can we have revival in our churches today? Yes — if Christians are willing to pray much, yield themselves to God, confess their sins, and let God have His way in their lives.

On my first missionary trip to Buenos Aires, Argentina, I found much division in one Russian-speaking church. I decided not to stay in anyone's home, but to rent a room in a hotel and spend some time in prayer. I wondered why I had to go to South America to pray for someone else's troubles and problems. Alone in that hotel room, I had a terrific burden for these people and was moved to fast and pray all night for revival among these Christians, so that God would break stubborn hearts and make people humble themselves and confess their sins.

Before I had come on this trip, one man had told me that I was wasting my time going to Buenos Aires or even praying. He said nothing could be done there because of the coldness, division and unforgiving spirit among Christians. Humanly speaking, that man was right. There was not much we could do. But we read in Mark 10:27, "Jesus looked at them and said, 'With men it is impossible, but not with God; for with God all things are possible.'" I stood on this promise, that God was able to move those hearts and send a revival — and the Lord answered my prayer in a wonderful way.

People from both sides of the division came to see me and tell me their side of the story, but I had only one thing to tell them: "Pray; get right with the Lord and with one another; humble yourselves; confess your sins." Many did not like this advice, but it was all I could tell them. Finally, with the Lord's help through prayer, the two groups of people agreed to come together for one service where I could talk to both of them. We first had an evangelistic service that lasted until 9:30 p.m. After this, we had another meeting, this time only for the Christians from the two divided groups, starting at 10:00 p.m.

About 11:30 that night, a real revival broke out among them. The leaders and other people from the divided groups started to cry out to God, asking Him for forgiveness. All of the people were on their knees in prayer. The next thing we knew, Christians were crawling on their knees to other Christians, putting their arms around them and asking forgiveness. There was much confession and repentance before God and before one another. There was weeping from sorrow and crying for joy, and this meeting continued until 1:30 a.m. People were praising the Lord and confessing their faults to one another for the problems and troubles they were experiencing.

How God answered prayer! When each Christian saw his own faults and saw that as an individual he was responsible for the troubles and divisions, he asked God for forgiveness. Soon the church was united and there was great victory and spiritual awakening that eventually spread to other churches in Argentina and Paraguay.

LIVING VICTORIOUSLY THROUGH PRAYER

We can have victory and live a very happy life if we meet the condition that is set forth in 1 John 3:22, "And whatever we ask we receive from Him, because we keep His commandments and do those things that are pleasing in His sight." When we fulfill God's will and keep His commandments, we are pleasing in His sight and our prayers are answered. "If you abide in Me, and My words abide in you, you will ask what you desire, and it shall be done for you" (John 15:7). As we are willing to do God's will and keep His commandments, our prayer life will take on new meaning and power so that we will be able to live victoriously. Only God can help us live the victorious life, and He will do that only as we are obedient to Him. The Holy Spirit must have full possession of our lives.

We can live victoriously, even in the midst of the wicked world. As Jesus prayed, "I have given them Your Word; and the world has hated them because they are not of the world, just as I am not of the world. I do not pray that You should take them out of the world, but that You should keep them from the evil one" (John 17:14-15). Jesus did not pray that we would be taken from the world, but rather that we should stay in the world and be a testimony. Although there will be temptations from the world, we are to resist them and die daily to them by the power of Him who lives within us to give us strength.

Paul said, "I have been crucified with Christ; it is no longer I who live, but Christ lives in me; and the life which I now live in the flesh I live by faith in the Son of God, who loved me and gave Himself for me" (Galatians 2:20). Isn't that wonderful? Paul was living, yet it was not he, but Christ living within him, giving him the strength to resist temptation and live victoriously. As we take time to commune with the One who lives within us and have fellowship with Him, we too will have the strength to live victoriously.

No matter what conditions we face, we know that Christ is the Victor. In Him, there is victory for you today. Matthew 5:6 promises, "Blessed are those who hunger and thirst for righteousness, for they shall be filled."

How I thank God that years ago I saw that Christ not only provided salvation on the cross for me, but He also provided victory over self, sin and the world. Romans 6:11 is a Scripture verse which has been a great blessing to me: "Likewise you also, reckon yourselves to be dead indeed to sin, but alive to God in Christ Jesus our Lord." Paul said, "I die daily." We must die daily. When I came from Russia in my youth, I could not speak English. I could only say, "Sure, all right." If anyone said anything to me or about me, it never bothered me because I was dead to the English language. My answer only was, "Sure, all right." A dead person is never disturbed by anything. We could speak well of him or against him, and it would be all the same to him because he is dead. If we are to live a victorious Christian life, we should be dead to our surroundings. We may meet opposition and criticism, but thank God we are not living for ourselves but for Him who died for us and rose victoriously from the dead.

I thank God that throughout all these years Christ has given me victory and I have lived a happy and blessed Christian life. In Christ Jesus I find peace, joy and rest in my soul. I have learned that the secret of living the victorious Christian life is staying in constant communion with the Lord through much prayer, thereby abiding in Him and having constant fellowship with the Lord.

EPILOGUE
BY Ruth Deyneka Erdel

Looking back over my life, I hold precious memories of my father, Peter Deyneka Sr., kneeling in prayer. With face lifted toward heaven, he prayed — *often!* Everything in our family and at Slavic Gospel Association was decided and accomplished through prayer.

He repeatedly acted out his favorite verse: "Call to Me, and I will answer you, and show you great and mighty things, which you do not know" (Jeremiah 33:3). I remember hearing him asking God for wisdom and strength to lead the mission. There were prayers for the health, safety and support of the missionaries. He longed to see more Scriptures and books printed, more Russian radio programs produced, and more churches built. But above all this, he had a great burden for more souls to be saved.

Upon his return home after an extended missionary journey, I remember how he gathered together dear Mama, sister Lydia, brother Peter and me to tell us about all the new opportunities for evangelism he had encountered. His prayers would intensify as he called on the Lord to send more missionaries and more funds in order to expand the ministry. I can still clearly recall his resounding voice reminding us that *much* prayer brings *much* power! There was also the sobering statement that *little* prayer resulted in *little* power.

What a privilege it was to travel to Europe with my father in July 1950. After a full summer of meetings held throughout many Russian refugee camps in Austria and Germany, Papa returned to America and I returned to Frankfurt, Germany, to begin my missionary work. The last thing we did together was to kneel by his bed aboard the *Queen Mary* and have prayer. That incident is still my inspiration today as I embark on missionary opportunities that continue to come my way.

Now, we must look to the future! There is so much to be done today for God's Kingdom: we must distribute more Bibles and Christian books; pastors and church leaders need training; funds are needed to complete church construction; people are going hungry. We have my father's example of taking all these needs to the Lord in prayer. Let us be encouraged by his motto: *Much Prayer — Much Power!* Let us do what we can to bring God's Word to some lost souls today.

SLAVIC GOSPEL ASSOCIATION

SGA is a global, nondenominational, evangelical mission organization, founded in 1934 by Peter Deyneka Sr., a Russian immigrant with a deep concern for the spiritual well-being of his compatriots wherever they were to be found. After the fall of the Iron Curtain, profound political and economic changes spread across the former Soviet Union and Central and Eastern Europe. Today, SGA's ministries are concentrated in these regions with the aim of serving the local, indigenous, evangelical churches to bring the Gospel of Jesus Christ to their own peoples. Through a unified strategy, SGA ministries in Australia, Canada, New Zealand, the United Kingdom and the United States work together to that end.

SGA carries out a multifaceted range of missionary outreach including media ministries (literature, radio and TV) based increasingly within the target countries themselves, training of nationals for pastoral ministries and church planting, sponsorship of church planters, pastor training conferences and youth camps, children's work, prison ministries, church construction assistance, and the provision of humanitarian aid which is distributed by the local churches. Regional ministry centers are maintained in Moscow (Russia), Minsk (Belarus), and Kiev (Ukraine) to support the outreach of national churches in the former Soviet Union.

In the fall of 1997, SGA accepted the invitation of the Union of Evangelical Christians-Baptists (UECB) of Russia to become their official representative in the United States, Australia, Canada and New Zealand. Training, equipping and supporting ministries are simultaneously taking place in Poland, the Czech and Slovak Republics, Hungary, Romania, Moldova, Bulgaria, Croatia, Serbia and Macedonia.

If you would like to learn more about SGA and its many ministries, please contact:

AUSTRALIA
Slavic Gospel Association
P.O. Box 396, Noble Park, Victoria 3174

CANADA
Slavic Gospel Association of Canada
55 Fleming Drive, Suite #26, Cambridge, Ontario N1T 2A9

NEW ZEALAND
Slavic Gospel Association
P.O. Box 10-156, 591 Dominion Road, Auckland 4

UNITED KINGDOM
Slavic Gospel Association
37A The Goffs, Eastbourne, East Sussex BN21 1HF

UNITED STATES
Slavic Gospel Association
6151 Commonwealth Drive, Loves Park, Illinois 61111